Tina Bruce is an author, yoga teacher, medical intuitive and retreat leader.

Tina spent the first 15 years of her working life in high pressure fast-paced roles within the medical industry. At the age of 31 Tina became a mother to two children in the space of one year.

Tina's entry into motherhood was marked by a quick return to work, followed by burnout, shingles and the development of an opioid addiction to manage the subsequent Post Herpetic Neuralgia (a chronic pain condition).

These events pushed Tina to embark on a Yoga journey to reconnect with her intuition and foster self-acceptance, self-healing and ultimately, recovery.

Tina holds an Advanced Diploma in Yoga from the Australian Yoga Academy. She is also a qualified Intuitive Coach from the Institute of Intuitive Intelligence.

Her first book, "Mother's Medicine: The Birth of My Intuition" is a memoir about this experience.

Tina now uses her own experience to assist other mothers to uncover and release subconscious fears that drain their energy and prevent them from reaching their full potential.

Tina regularly hosts intimate Yin Yoga classes and spiritual retreats and offers private one on one coaching.

She lives in Melbourne with her husband and two daughters.

MOTHER'S MEDICINE

THE BIRTH OF MY INTUITION

AUTHOR'S NOTE

This book is a memoir. It reflects my recollections and opinions of particular experiences over time. Some names have been changed to protect the privacy of individuals and some events have been compressed or dramatised for the sake of the narrative.

This book contains information about my personal journey and is no way intended to be a substitute for professional medical advice.

DISCLAIMER

Cover design and book design © 2019 Hannah Sutton Design
www.hannahsuttondesign.com
Editor - Vanessa Barrington (The Right Remark)
www.therightremark.com
Illustrations © 2019 Hannah Sutton Design
Author photograph by Prue Aja www.prueaja.com.au

CONTENTS

For the loves of my life:
Oliver, my rock
Leila and Zoe, my two miracles

INTRODUCTION

The definition of the Mother Archetype is the giver of life at the cosmic and human levels. She is gentle and fierce; a lioness when required. She's a caregiver to all. She desires to help and protect others. She is that which sustains and nurtures. Her intuitive power is this medicine.

The moment a woman gives birth to her baby she also gives birth to her own medicine. Her intuition. Whether she welcomes it or not, she is initiated with her own 'Mother's Medicine' designed to heal, restore and grow life in and around her. It is an energetic psychic wonder that only the physical link gets severed when the umbilical cord is cut. In every other non-physical way, she stays connected to a force with great potential.

Contrary to what many people believe, intuition is not a gift - it is programmed in all of us. Most of us have simply become very good at blocking it, or found that it lays dormant until some significant event, crisis or life change activates its power.

Intuition is like buried treasure in the depths of a woman's body. The pain (or non-pain) of childbirth so often becomes the event that triggers the unearthing of this treasure. It pushes a mother out of her head and into the present moment as she feels a mind blowing connection with the divine energy or pure unconditional love. The highest vibration of all universal energies.

On the other hand, I know some mothers whose description of their post birth initiation was not quite like this. They share their war stories about wanting to sneak out of hospital in the depths of the night, between breast feeds and night nurse shift swaps. They dream of floating past the nurses' station and out into the car park.

"Let me pretend this tiny human doesn't exist," they think.

"Please return me to my old life where I can sleep uninterrupted for as long as I like."

Intuition is sneaky like that. Often you don't even realise it's just hiding and patiently waiting in the wings until you're ready to respond. Some of us need a sweetener, a spoonful of sugar or something extra to help the medicine go down. Your sweetener will be unique to you and it's usually something that helps us grow into motherhood. For me, that thing was Yoga but there are a variety of vehicles which deliver spiritual sweetness. As long as they get you there it doesn't matter what route they take.

When I was pregnant for the first time I thought about what sort of mother I was going to be. I definitely thought about all the possible names I would call my child and considered carefully how I would come to those decisions. I started studying books and reading magazines and browsing homeware stores, as I planned on how to decorate the baby's bedroom, what type of pram to buy and all the rest of it. I went through a nesting stage preparing my home for a seemingly smooth transition into motherhood. I chatted about it endlessly with my friends. I went to birthing classes and carefully researched and investigated all my options for delivery. I held a carefully constructed birth plan in my hands. I even visualised holding my baby close to my chest and feeding effortlessly on my breast like a natural earth mama. I was thrown a traditional baby shower where all the gifts, consumable cuteness, and parenting advice designed to last me a lifetime was abstractly squeezed into one single afternoon tea.

None of it prepared me for what was actually going to happen.

My reality of motherhood was completely different to what I expected. What I wasn't prepared for, was that my 'idea' around being a mother was nothing close to the truth. People tried to describe to me what it was and how it felt, but it didn't come close to the actual experience. Perhaps I should have titled this book: 'What *Not* to Expect When You Are Expecting'.

My two children were born by caesarian section (C-section), but were two very different experiences. My first birth was a traumatic circus. You know how clowns are meant to make you smile but instead they are all too commonly terrifying and scary? I felt like I was surrounded by crazy clowns. My second birth was more like a classical orchestra performance. Beautifully rehearsed and controlled, pitch and note perfect at the hands of a fine tuned conductor. An elective C-section with a different doctor, different instruments, different hospital and accompanied by a completely pain-free melody.

Regardless of delivery method, both births produced the same outcomes; two little miracles. I wasn't prepared for the speed at which I could comprehend these were, in fact, miracles. Why is birth so amazing? I mean, if this is what we are here for, why are we so amazed every single time we produce a human? It was impossible for me to predict that I would feel the level of love I did. When my babies were placed cheek to cheek with me, I automatically understood the potency of my new perception. It didn't take me any time to learn it. It was an instant *knowing* at the speed of light otherwise called my intuition or, as I also like to call it, my 'Mother's Medicine'.

Your intuition is strategically layered and reveals itself to you in stages, just like the three stages of labour in childbirth. These include your functional gut intuition or 'First Stage Intuition'. This original layer is literally how you are wired as an animal to survive. For example, your *fight or flight* instinct is not something you need to develop. Just like in early labour, you are going through the motions of ensuring you are in a safe environment and managing your way through contractions relatively routinely. At this stage, your intuition's job is to alert you that something is happening without you needing to really think about it.

The next level of intuition is the manifestation layer or 'Second Stage Intuition'. It requires a great level of trust and presence, as you don't know what the outcome of the birth will be, but you realise you have some influence. It is here that you become creative with your body and your breathing. You might try several positions, add in some water or a bath, try some drugs, rest in between contractions, or recruit a coach to help manage your pain. You really start to heighten your physical senses as to what *feels* right and you allow your emotions to flow. This is the stage where you may be able to change your own reality through your choices, according to what is true. Your power is an active force, rather than something that passively receives fate. You are creating your destiny.

The 'Third Stage Intuition' or psychic intuition is the final layer which is revealed or unveiled to you. At this level a connection to something greater than you makes itself known. Your baby is born! The initiation into the final layer of the intuitive mother is downloaded the instant the baby comes out. One moment you are experiencing pregnant motherhood and labour over a gradual nine-month horizontal period, week by week, day by day, and the next second you have been vertically hit on the head with a profound power that exists beyond time and space.

You are in a mystical state of bliss because there is no boundary between you and the true nature of the universe; unconditional love. You are experiencing the building block of life in its purest energetic form. There is no such thing as *doubt* when you are staring the infinite in the face. One of the messages you often receive from loved ones after you send out the birth announcement is 'He/She is *perfect*', or 'how *divine*'.

That's because this is exactly what miracles are. Finding the right words and language to wrap around this, to express the magnitude of the reality, is almost impossible.

Each labour stage requires a different level of commitment from you; a different level of trust in your own personal power. Intuition is not about crystal balls, outsourcing your power to tarot readers or predicting the future. It's about creating a comfort zone with yourself to absorb the truth in the present moment. The truth being that we are way more powerful than we believe (if only we could trust it).

There are countless demonstrations of mother's intuition being the most natural knowing we possess as the divine feminine race. For example, when your toddler is walking behind you and wanders into traffic. You don't need eyes in the back of your head, you simply *know* she is heading for danger and you selflessly leap to protect that child without needing time to think about it. In the same way, we hear cases of women lifting cars to free their trapped child pinned underneath; almost turning themselves inside out, willing to do anything (including die) for their little miracle. When you become a mother, your mind is blown into a new awareness. This new head space is not based on fact or logic. Rather, the doorway into understanding your intuition is through the heart brain which breeds an irrational love and devotion.

Nobody usually mentions how you will be reborn in the process of becoming a mother because our culture focuses so strongly on the child and how to be a perfect parent.

This book is about my journey to understand how incredibly powerful I am and how fast this connection to my own intuition alleviated pain and suffering and helped me to raise a resilient family. It's a book about living my spiritual truth out loud and becoming my own healer by taking my own medicine. We can all learn to become better humans through the experience of motherhood and the deep love and protection we feel for our children.

Yoga is the vehicle through this exploration as each pose offers the space to experience being a 'whole' person in an empowering new way. With the guidance of intuition, my journey required me to be '*Self*-ish'. It required *Self* Love, *Self* Esteem and *Self* Acceptance. The exact three forces that mothers offer their children unconditionally (but often deny themselves). It is a story about treating ourselves as mothers with tenderness, understanding and compassion. It's about learning to let go of the negativity and replace those feelings with positive emotions. It should be easy, but it isn't. However, when you have children looking up to you for guidance, you realise loving your authentic self is the best gift you can give them.

It is only with hindsight (and a lot of courage!) that I have the ability to write my story. I am risking rejection by being honest, but I have no other option as you will soon understand. During the past decade, I have experienced many different types of pain and I feel I have been pregnant with this book for a while now. Acute, traumatic, chronic and ongoing are all the different types of pain that have supercharged my intuition. As women we call upon our intuition as our own medicine to know our own truth and live from an authentic place. To make choices aligned with our heart. To let go of any preconceived notions of what the 'perfect mother' looks like. To let old parts of the self die so the day a baby is born, a new mother is born also.

CHAPTER 1

GREEN MEANS GO!

Life's a journey not a race

Code Green*! Code Green! What does that mean? Suddenly the delivery suite begins to buzz and there is a palpable sense of 'oh shit' in the air. People moving everywhere fast. The midwife reports:

"Note, it's 1:30am, you are going to theatre."

My baby's heart rate has plummeted. The doctor is holding the skin from the baby's scalp in his hands after removing the vacuum from my vagina.

In my experience, it is never a good sign when doctors and nurses run. They look a bit like air stewards; displaying a neutral manner during fierce turbulence. Measured steps forward and an unwavering focus on business. I see their deadpan faces slip into worry and I start to panic. I have been labouring for 36 hours and I'm getting nowhere, fast. My hospital bed is being wheeled to the theatre as the staff surrounding me start running. Again, medics that run? Not good. I feel like I am in an episode of

* A code green in medical emergencies is described by the Victorian Emergency Guidelines as when there is an impending death or risk of the patient dying. When a code green is called all the team members attend the operating theatre and the patient is transported to theatre immediately. The average time for a code green to arrive in theatre is four minutes. When responding to emergencies any opportunity for error or lack of team work is amplified in the context of the reduced time frames.

ER except there is no George Clooney in sight. I fly down the corridor writhing in the full pain of labour contractions. They are so intense. The waves. So many waves, that just won't stop. I lose control of my legs as the bed rolls into the elevator and kick a nurse in the head. The sliding elevator doors open and I see the doors of the theatre swing wide. There's a crowd of around 20 staff waiting for me in the room. I feel an overwhelming sensation of being alone.

My husband Oliver is told to wait outside. He does not accept this direction so they give him some scrubs to change into. I am lifted and transferred like a flailing whale out of water onto the operating table as my sense of survival kicks in. Amidst the agony of the contractions I pick up words like 'severe bradycardia distress', 'high risk', 'head trauma' and 'hurry up'. I hear the machines alarming at the sound of my baby's heart rate plummeting.

"YES. Please hurry the hell up and give me something for this pain!" I think.

A drape is placed over my naked body as I lay on the operating table. I am completely at the mercy of these 'professionals'.

"Will my unborn child survive? Is this normal?"

Before this moment it was so easy to imagine the scenario of becoming a mother, but I sure didn't have this in my birth plan. My baby is stuck and her resistance to join me on the outside is causing incomprehensible chaos. There is no time to feel disappointed about not having a natural birth. My brain can't control or understand what is happening to my body. I completely switch into the most primal state of high alert and am focused on just one thing – survival. I hear mammalian grunts and growls and realise they are coming from me. I bounce between fighting, fleeing and freezing. Now *this* is pain. It is the fire before the actual fire of my baby emerging.

I see the surgeon walk in, scrubbed, gloves on and ready to go. I wonder where my obstetrician is as it registers that the man behind the mask is not my chosen doctor, the one I have paid the last nine months to prepare me for this very moment. I am in too much pain to talk or even formulate this question as I continue to try and make sense of what is going on. The contractions are unstoppable and excruciating and seem to have a mind of their own. An anaethetist stands at my right shoulder. She is wearing a badge labelled 'Resident'. I will later discover that a resident is a name for a trainee anaesthetist. I recognise the stunned expressions on the faces of the other 'doctors' watching the spectacle as students in training. They are observing on the outer edges of the room and taking notes.

"Please make this agony stop," I think.

There is no time to catch my breath in between contractions.

"Help me!" I gasp.

She is reaching for the syringe and about to load me up, knock me out and sedate me.

"Control the patient," I hear someone yell out. Instantly I feel weight bearing down on my arms and legs and hear the clicks of straps locking me in. At last I feel a cold sensation in my arm as the pain relieving medicine goes in the IV and into my veins. The noise and cacophony in the room quietens in anticipation. The doctor asks for his first instrument. A scalpel. My baby's life is in his hands. My life is in his hands. He is poised and ready and I am still very very aware. His hands lower onto my belly. They are cold. I can feel the cold. I can't see with the screen up in front of my face but without warning I feel a sharp sting.

"Faaarck!" I yell. Then nothing. Then again, a longer hot burning slice across my stomach. I am screaming.

"Ahhhhh! I can feel it!" I scream. His skinny bloodshot eyes squint above his mask and over the screen at me. He glares next to me at the anaesthetist.

"What did you give her?" he demands.

The realisation that I am experiencing my abdomen being

cut open sets in. The sparkling steel plunges into my belly. I am beyond a state of panic. I'm in a nightmare! I feel invisible. The air is thick with confusion. For a few seconds the intellects in the room are quizzically exchanging information across my body with their eyes. That squinty laser-like glance penetrates the anaesthetist as they try and work out why the epidural is failing. And then what happens next is surreal.

The doctor shakes his head and pauses for a moment. His words are clear and direct and they land on me like a slap.

"I can not wait." The ringmaster has spoken and the performance act begins.

The anaesthetist looks down at me. There is fear in her face.

"Look at me Tina, Tina look in my eyes," she begs as she clutches at my hand. There are sounds of metal clanking and I feel my insides exposed to cold air. It is as if I am turned inside out. My heart is galloping like it is trying to outrun the threat of being chased by a lion except I am the only wild animal in the room. While my blood pressure and stress levels climb further, I thrash in the straps and a team of staff rush to the bed to physically hold me down and restrain me.

Oliver is sitting behind my head watching the terror unfold. "Will my wife be ok?" he asks. Nobody replies. It appears my baby is the first priority. Later, I will recall that neither of us were given a choice in the matter. But in this moment I don't think about this. I only know the instrument in his right hand as it begins cutting through skin, veins, arteries, flesh and nerves until he finds my uterus. I am in agony. I feel everything. The next thing I experience is tugging and pulling of hands inside me. I feel like I am being gutted like a fish. The digging and rummaging seems to go on forever as I lie there on the operating table being disemboweled all the way up to my ribcage. Whatever the doctor is doing to me on the other side of the curtain is rough and feels violent. It is the most sickening sensation; much worse than the actual knife. One continuous long scream during the whole excruciating torture resounds over and over. I realise it's me making this terrible noise. I tremble from the gore and distaste at the surgeon's willingness to inflict such murderous intrusion on my body.

This is definitely happening. There is that strange out of body feeling of looking down on myself while observing what is actually going on. The pain becomes separate from me. Later, I remember thinking I knew absolutely nothing of the meaning of the word *pain* before that moment. Anything I thought was painful prior to this was merely a bad period.

"Look at me Tina", the anaesthetist keeps saying. The room begins to go fuzzy. I am fading. In shock. I want out. I know that if the agony at this intensity continues, it will kill me. I need to exit this reality, but I force my eyelids to stay open and press my fingernails as hard as I can into my palms. I can not give in to the pain pulling me under, knowing it wants to drown me. There is a baby I intuitively need to be here for. I am completely possessed. I am afloat, at sea. I am my own coast guard. I keep my eyes open and my head above water even though I physically want to sink like a leaky boat to the bottom of the ocean. And then I hear a cry. Suddenly something shifts and a wave of numbness and delusion washes over me as the drugs kick in. Just like that, it's like my boat shifts gear. The euphoria takes the edge off and the pain disappears. I feel a flood of relief through the drug haze as I hear the sound of a newborn baby's first cry. I don't even think to ask if it is a boy or a girl.

2am. Monday 12 April 2010.

The first glimpse of my baby suddenly rises above the curtain screen. I try to lift my arms and reach out to grab the slippery wriggly body even as the surgeon orders

"Don't move Tina, stay very still!"

The baby is swiftly taken to the corner of the room and checked over quickly for normal signs of life. The universe seems to tilt on its axis as the group gravitates to the corner of the room, concerned. I lie on the operating table, empty and hollow.

Finally, a man greets me.

"Meet your baby girl" he says. He presents her to me all wrapped up. I feel her cheek press up against mine and a huge sense of relief floods my senses. Her face is all swollen and squishy and blue and purple. Her entire head is one giant bruise peeking out from behind her swaddle. I carefully pull the swaddle back from her forehead. Her scalp is red raw and bleeding; she is covered in skin lacerations. The trauma on her head is from the failed vacuum delivery when the doctor attempted to turn her. I notice the midwife shooting daggers at the doctor as she sees the baby's head. There is muttering under her face mask and an exchange of looks amongst the nurses in the room. Looks of disgust and disrespect dart around in shared glances. They are all looking at my baby with great concern and care. I get the sense in my drug induced haze that this is familiar territory for these silently fierce women. A softer blanket is wrapped around my baby. Someone offers to take a photo of the three of us. Our new little family.

I look at my baby's face as her eyes blink open for the first time and life suddenly possesses her. Through the windows of her soul, I witness her consciousness come online as the spark of connection strikes her. At the same time as she *awakes* I feel new life *awaken* inside of me. She appears peaceful. Angelic, in spite of the fact she has already experienced so much pain entering the world. She is alive and beautiful and I melt into a morphine-infused new mother moment. Oliver and I had the name Zara picked out for a girl, but it doesn't seem to match.

'Leila' is the name we decide in that moment. I later will discover it means '*Dark beauty of the night*'.

The following morning after my screwed up c-section, I'm lying in the ward all swollen with fluids. The sharpness in my abdomen is fresh and severe. My obstetrician who was away for the weekend comes to my bedside at 7am.

"Where the hell were you yesterday?" I think angrily. I go to make the words but can't seem to move my mouth in the drug-infused haze. He looks at me and no words are required from me.

"I'm sorry I wasn't there for you," he apologises.

"The doctor who delivered Leila was actually my *much more* experienced colleague. Next time we will do an elective caesarian", he says matter-of-factly.

"Next time? Wow..." I think to myself.

"The problem was that the baby's head was fully stuck in a posterior position making a natural delivery impossible. I personally would have ordered you a c-section straight away and not have attempted a natural," he continues.

"Well that's very helpful," I think sarcastically.

All the same, he just keeps talking. Bantering on – talking about a segment of me, focusing on what he does best.

"The problem was that Leila's spine was actually running along your spine and her face was looking up at the sky wedging the widest part of her head in your birth canal. I'm sorry you've had a horrible time but feel grateful your baby is alive, enjoy this moment," he says.

I am lost for words.

"All that matters is a healthy baby at the end of the day," says a nurse as she appears at my side to take my blood pressure. I try and sit up so I can look at Leila's face but I move upright too fast and vomit instead. I wonder how to turn the ghastly into something good again.

***

I wake up on day three, not knowing it is day three. I don't actually know what day of the week it is. I don't know if it is day or night, Monday or Thursday. I just know that I have woken up, unsure if I am asleep or dozing or dreaming. I can hardly lift my head from the pillow. I am dutifully dosed up on strong opiate drugs to manage my acute post-surgical pain. The drugs are conveniently fading my memory of the birth. Someone thrusts the baby in my arms and says it is time to feed again. I'm sure I did this only five minutes ago but my concept of time has gone out the window. I obey. I do what I'm told because my body clock is no longer reliable. I feel a throbbing in my chest and notice my boobs are up around my neck. A nurse appears.

"Your milk has come in", she says.

"You should try and get up and go to the bathroom. I'll go and fetch the pump and we'll see if we can express and bottle some of that." I am a cow being milked at the whim of a revolving door of milk maids who demand I produce. The nurse leaves on her mission to retrieve the pails.

My feet hit the floor and gravity shifts from a horizontal landscape to a vertical drop. My insides fall into new pockets and spaces inside my abdomen. My organs have found new real estate and I'm a foreigner inside my own body. It's like someone has entered my house in the middle of the night and rearranged all the furniture. Finding my way through the dark, I search for familiar senses and look for something to hold onto. Something secure and solid. There is a peculiar detachment to this flesh suit I'm breathing inside of. I need a torch or someone to shine a light inside and reassure me so I can see that I am indeed upright in my own body. But I don't trust the strangers who run in and out of the room to keep me safe.

A robber usually waits until people go away on holidays to break in and steal what doesn't belong to them. I must stay vigilant and on guard. My body is my home, after all, and is wired with all alarm sensors turned on. Confined to a private room I have no neighbours within view to watch out for suspect behavior in the hood. I shuffle over to the clipboard at the end of my bed. Each movement pulls on a stitch in a wobbly stomach wound so deep I have to place my hands on top to prevent my insides falling out. I pick up the clipboard which holds my patient notes in place.

'Christina Bruce',
DOB 09/02/79,
Age 31.

15/04/10
Day three

Patient pain management; Tramadol every four hours, Endone every six hours

Comments; blank

"Blank?"

I look at the space where there should be words and details about patient management. I glance out the door at the nurses and midwives who move and overtake each other like passing ships in the night. There is a constant flow of different staff.

"Who is responsible for the patient notes?" I wonder. I notice more gaps in the paperwork so pick up the pen and write down the time: 11:30am. Tramadol 100mg. colostrum expressed 50ml.

Someone has spelled Leila's name incorrectly. I cross out

Layla and write her name again, correctly. 'Leila'.

Ollie looks up from the newspaper.

"It's not your job to fill out the patient charts" he says.

"I know but nobody is doing it," I reply annoyed.

I continue to write and notice more gaps. I'm writing an essay now, analysing this document and even punctuating the sentences. I look down at my swollen belly and catch a glimpse of my purple feet. My legs begin to shake and I feel my very foundation start to collapse from underneath me. I grab a hold of the bed rail and sit down, still clutching the clipboard with one hand.

Ollie shakes his head.

"Stop it, please put down the clipboard."

I place the clipboard next to the bed so it is within easy reach and I can update it with bits of new data. I feel very tired all of a sudden and I ask Ollie to take Leila down to the nursery so I can have a little nap. Suddenly he has a job to do. He jumps up purposefully, wheeling her out of the room and across the hall. I watch her bruised scabbed head roll out the door. Anyone would think I had dragged her by the feet along a bitumen highway. I glance at the bedside table over my bed to make sure the clipboard crying out to me stays exactly where it is.

The next day I am allowed visitors and my mother is the first waiting on the ward to see me and meet her precious grandchild. I have never been as relieved to see anyone as I am her.

For a brief moment when she enters the room I feel like everything will be ok. She has a look of compassion and pure love on her face. Our intuitive bond is as strong as ever and I sense she can feel my pain but is being strong for both of us. She picks up Leila and cuddles her close while sitting down in the arm chair opposite my bed, meeting her newborn granddaughter for the first time and breathing in the pure innocent smell of her essence.

The last time I spoke with Mum was the day I went into labour at 39 weeks. I was having labour pains at home and everything was progressing smoothly and as expected. Naturally after receiving the news of my experience the pressing question on her lips is

"Tina... What happened?"

I take a deep breath and tell her my story.

***

It was Saturday morning and I woke up as usual, early and quite excited to start the weekend. There were a few things I had on my list to get done before the baby was technically due. I wasn't expecting anything to happen any earlier for my first pregnancy. I had arranged to go for a walk around the lake and then meet my best friend for brunch after. I'm still not sure how I walked or waddled four kilometres being that large but I was actually relatively fit and kept pretty active throughout my pregnancy. I met Maggie at 10am at a little café close by and we chatted excitedly about the impending birth and if I thought it would be a boy or a girl and what names were on the shortlist. We chatted and carried on until our avocado on toast arrived to the table and was placed in front of us.

I took one bite of my toast and then for some reason couldn't eat anymore. My appetite had disappeared, like someone switching off a light. I immediately felt tired and the thought of food made me feel a little sick. Not surprisingly, I was at the stage where a morning nap was not out of the question so I left the café and went home only to jump straight back into bed. It was only 11am, but I felt like I had been hit by a truck. It was effortless to pass out and drift straight into sleep.

Three hours later I woke up wondering what time it was. I went to the bathroom and noticed a very strange mucous-y alien-like blob fall out of me.

"Ahhh," I thought.

"That must be 'the plug' they refer to which sits on your cervix holding baby inside."

Literally pulling the plug out, I wondered what might drain out of me. Nothing happened except in my mind I knew a shift had taken place and maybe this was the start of early labour. A few hours later and my first contraction started while lying on the couch watching TV. Excited, I told Ollie that it was getting closer. For dinner we ordered Indian take away and I ate some spicy tandoori chicken in the hope it would move things along. It seemed to work, as by the time dinner had finished my contractions were around five minutes apart. They felt totally manageable and I rang the hospital to let them know. The nurse on the phone said to just stay where I was, take two Panadeine and go to bed. I followed her instructions and didn't feel like I would be able to sleep but did manage to get a few hours and breathed through the contractions overnight. By around 11am the next day things were starting to get quicker and more intense so I rang the hospital and told them I was coming in.

Once I arrived I discovered my obstetrician was not available so we were assigned a different doctor. Perhaps this was just the unlucky nature of going into labour on Sunday bloody Sunday. You get whoever is rostered on-call for that weekend, even though you just spent the previous six months building a relationship with an entirely different person. Somebody who knows you intimately, understands your history, your fears and your partner. The professional you paid to listen to your birth plan, your potential baby names and your blood pressure. Instead I lifted my head and gazed tentatively in front of me.

"Hello there stranger who I have never met before staring intently in between my legs..." I thought.

He knelt down and did an exam and said that I was only 1cm

dilated.

"Damn," I thought.

"So much work ahead of me."

I should have turned around and gone back home at this stage. I had no idea how long this process would take. But then as the doctor looked up and peeled off his gloves one by one he delivered the news, or should I say the weather and said:

"I'm going to break your waters."

Intervention number one.

He left for about an hour and came back holding what looked like a knitting needle in his hands. Awkwardly, the man whose face I had only met once, dove right back down to take another look.

"Still only 1cm," he confirmed. He could have been reporting rainfall measurements. He inserted a long steel tool between my legs. It felt cold even though on the outside I was dripping with perspiration. I heard a 'pop' sound and then felt like I had peed my pants as he ruptured the amniotic sac. Looking at his face I could tell he was tired and over it. His ginger hair disheveled; wispy bits blowing under the ceiling fan across his face. His shirt had food stains on it and held the evidence of what looked like his last several meals down the front. More fluid continued to pour out of me as he signaled to the midwife to tidy up the sheets.

"That should do it. It's been a busy weekend, I've delivered six babies so far this weekend. Your baby will be lucky number seven if it arrives this evening," he said.

I wasn't sure whether 'lucky' is how I should feel coming last in the line up of a 48 hour shift.

So after the waterfall, I continued to have contractions, moving around and bouncing through them on the fit ball. I was talking with anyone who walked into the room to distract me, chatting away freely and even telling the odd joke. I was beginning to get suspicious at my own boredom and ability to hold a conversation while in labour. The doctor returned about three hours later and did another exam. Same news.

"You're only 1cm dilated," he said.

I was starting to feel like I was doing a marathon but on a treadmill.

"Why is nothing happening," I thought.

"Am I doing it wrong?"

At this point it was getting dark outside and we were approaching the evening shift of staff handover. He looked up at me slightly breathless and said:

"We will induce you with Syntocin and we recommend an epidural at the same time to manage the pain." Being my first pregnancy I didn't know what the timeline or speed of labour was. Sure, I was frustrated and impatient but I wasn't overdue...I was 39 weeks.

Intervention number 2.

I studied the doctor's face as he searched the hallway and room for a familiar face. The anaethetist at this private hospital was about to go home for the evening so I sensed the doctor's urgency to get an epidural in me before he left the building. The anaethetist came in syringe ready, and explained all the risks and procedure to administer the epidural. I sat very still on the bed as he stuck the big needle in my spine.

"This will only hurt for a second, just try not to move," he instructed as I was infused with a drug. I was told that in around fifteen minutes I would be numb from the waist down. It was duly administered and I remember the bliss as the pain receded to the end of what felt like a very long tunnel.

In my left arm an IV was inserted and I was hooked up to a drip which leaked the Syntocin into my system to speed the labour along. Being fully bedbound, I was told to relax and wait. I remember eating lollies and watching episodes of a Melbourne gangster show on TV feeling absolutely nothing.

"This is great," I thought. I lay there dilating as fast as I could shoving jelly beans into my mouth. In a couple of hours I had reached 10cm and had no idea until I was told it was time to push.

"What, I'm 10cm already?" I asked dumbfounded.

"Yep, wakey time, you need to focus now, it's time to do some work" the midwife ordered sharply.

Being instructed on how to give birth when you can't really feel anything from the waist down is a bit like walking around blindfolded. I was relying totally on her instructions and doing what I was told. It felt totally unnatural and not what I imagined having a baby would feel like. I pictured myself down on all fours grunting and moaning and rocking and rolling - but not this.

"You're not pushing properly, you need to really focus and try to time it with the contractions," the midwife said.

I didn't enjoy failing at anything so her comments got under my skin a bit.

"You need to stop topping up the epidural medicine and back off the pain relief so you can feel the contractions and bear down. You're not doing it properly," she said.

Over the next hour the sensations in my feet and legs returned and I could feel the pain being revealed like someone was lifting a veil from the lower half of my body. Being a 'good patient' and not wanting to disappoint, I stopped the self-administering epidural and for a brief moment felt like a brave woman doing it naturally. At this point she then ordered my husband - pointing at him.

"You! I need your help, come over here and hold a leg." Ollie jumped out of his seat and followed her direction. It was not my desire for him to go down the business end, but again, we were just following instructions and starting to freak out at the bossy midwife. He did a good job coaching me and took his role as 'leg holder' very seriously. Suddenly, we were alarmed by the sound of the foetal monitor. The baby's heart rate was slowing down and becoming erratic. Two hours of pushing and no progress was starting to cause some major distress and heart rate variation. The doctor swaggered into the room like he had just hopped off his trusty steed. Removing the ventouse (a vacuum-like device) from his holster, he was armed and ready for a lasoo-like extraction.

Intervention number three.

I was now in some serious pain. The contractions were coming thick and strong but this was not altering my ability to push the baby out any better. The position of the baby's head was making it difficult for it to descend out through the birth canal. The doctor attached the ventouse cap to her skull inside me and said,

"I'm going to try and pull the baby now."

The pain in that moment was indescribable. The pulling and the pressure of the head was so intense I was losing confidence and in shock. It was at this point that the contractions were so strong and constant I lost control. I regretted not topping myself up with the epidural.

"Why did I listen to that nurse?" I thought. I looked down and saw beads of sweat rolling down the doctor's red and flushed face. The foetal heart monitor was alarming continually now. He looked stressed and defeated. What felt like hours later, he finally pulled his hand out of me. In his fingers he was holding the skin from my baby's scalp.

Intervention number four.

His response was immediate.
"Code Green!" he ordered.
Then everything spun out of control.

***

"Why didn't you tell me birth was so horrendous and traumatic Mum!? There was no warning written anywhere in *What to expect when you are expecting*."

My mother had two natural births and positive experiences with both kids, so there was no precautionary advice from her.

I stayed in hospital for five days and then was sent home. I wasn't ready, but I knew it was longer than most women were allowed to stay. As my body was divinely designed, the pain memory of the birth faded as the oxytocin hormones kicked in and I moved on with the business of breastfeeding and getting to know my child. The memory slightly faded but was not forgotten.

After Leila was born, the doctor gave me strict instructions to continue to take the opioid painkiller pills so I could be as comfortable as possible in my recovery. In order to control the pain and create some order in the chaos, I followed these instructions and medicated myself. I liked the Tramadol not just because it took the post-surgical discomfort away but it also made me feel more calm, capable and confident. I was desperately trying to hold on to some sense that I was still in control. I wanted to believe that the magic pills would keep me safe so that nothing was too scary or overwhelming or too much. It filled a gap and made me feel what I imagined being a mother should feel like. The drug made me feel natural.

After the bloody event was done and dusted, the welcome baby gifts unwrapped, and congratulation flowers had started to wilt, the real labour at home began.

It was relentless, round the clock, thankless, unpaid, crazy god damn hard work. The pills gave me more energy to do the housework in between feeding and being social when visitors popped by for a visit. I remember feeling disappointed when I took the last one in the packet and my scar was healing as expected.

"The power in these little pills is so strong," I pondered. I could see how heroin addicts and street junkies might find themselves hooked, but did not think for one second that opiate addiction doesn't discriminate.

My cravings for the drugs at home became stronger and stronger. It surprised me how much the focus was on the actual birth for a mother while she was pregnant, and not what happened afterwards as an actual parent. It was challenging adjusting to our new family, to say the least. I threw myself into the role by trying to control when the baby would eat and sleep. I put Leila on a strict routine and made her sleep in her own cot and her own room from the moment we arrived home. It made me feel more confident when I could predict and manage the events of the day. Sometimes I even forgot that she was a human being and not a robot. I would find myself getting frustrated if she dared to veer from the program and change her habits. I even got frustrated with my lack of control over my milk production so breastfeeding pretty quickly turned into bottle feeding. It was detachment parenting at its best except that I was overly in love and overly protective of her. In spite of this controlling behavior, I never deprived her of love and cuddles, to the point that I wouldn't let anyone else hold her but me. If I tried to pass her over to a friend or family member she would scream the house down. I wanted to feel like a natural easygoing mother but instead I felt insecure and frighteningly rigid.

One of the most common pieces of advice I received during this time is to 'nap when your baby naps'. The only problem is when *she* sleeps, I *can't* sleep. I don't think too much about the birthing experience but my body feels tense and anxious. I'm wired and awake even though I feel tired. All the time. I am adjusting to this new little life, this new identity and wondering exactly if I am doing it right.

***

After a few months Leila is already starting to sleep through the night, which is technically at least a six hour stretch of time. You would think I would be over the moon by this fact, however, I wake up each day and can't seem to shake the nervousness. I constantly feel an anxiety humming along in the background somewhere deep inside my body. I vigilantly monitor Leila's sleep and nap time schedule. I set timers on my phone to remind me what I should be doing and when. I continually feel sick in my stomach and foggy in my head hoping this is all just a virus that will pass. Intuitively I know that I need to get away and have a change of scene. I call the first person who will understand.

"Mum, I'm coming up to Brisbane and bringing Leila with me for a few days. I need a break."

I arrive at Brisbane airport after my first plane trip together with Leila. She finally falls asleep as we are landing. Outside the gate, my mother stands waiting for us, smiling. Straight away I hand Leila over into Nanny's open arms as I desperately run to the closest toilet to relieve my bursting bladder. I have held on for more than two hours, too afraid to pass her on to a steward, knowing she would scream and upset all the other passengers.

"'I feel like I'm going to be sick," I say to Mum as I emerge from the bathrooms.

"Why don't we get you home and I'll cook you a nice homemade roast. You need a good meal and a rest by the looks of things," she says, eyeing me carefully.

The smell of the Queensland warm air is familiar and soothing. We walk to the car where she has a baby seat fitted and ready for her granddaughter. I can tell she is happy we are both here but I can also sense her concern for my wellbeing, as only a mother can. She intuitively knows something is off.

We get home and settle in and Leila is happy playing on the floor on her rug. She is starting to hold and grab things in her hands, entertaining herself with her own cleverness. Mum and I float over her, adoring her warbling noises and sweet coos as we listen to all the new sounds coming out of her pursed lips. I get up to help Mum prepare dinner and am hit by a smell that sends a wave of nausea through me. She is holding the leg of lamb in her hands and rubbing it with oil and spices.

"Geez, I don't feel so good," I murmur. I put down my glass of wine – suddenly unable to sip another mouthful and walk to the bedroom to sit down. A wave of frustration and sadness hits me. I am losing the ability to enjoy the simple pleasures of life. My mum's intuitive radar goes off.

"Could you be pregnant?"

"What? No way, I highly doubt it. What are you talking about Mum?" I say.

The last time the gamey stench of lamb made me feel like puking was when I was pregnant. I can't even remember the last time I had sex with my husband in my sleep deprived state. Leila is only four months old - it's not as if there has been much time.

I did get my period back six weeks after the birth which I thought was quite soon but I haven't been keeping track of my cycle at all. I recall someone saying to me that when a baby sleeps through the night quite early you begin to miss a feed overnight; and that can be just enough to kick your hormones back into gear.

I look up at Mum, eyes widening. She put her arms around me.

"Why don't you go and get a test in the morning just for peace of mind," she says.

The next morning I go straight to the pharmacy and buy three tests. I go back to the house and lock myself in the bathroom. I pee on six sticks.

Positive, positive, positive, positive, positive and positive. Fuck.

Savasana

Savasana Pose

Savasana or *Corpse Pose* is usually done at the end of a Yoga practice and looks like the easiest shape but is actually the most difficult. For me, it was the start of a long and slow death of my old self. While it appears restful, falling asleep was not the goal. It marked the beginning of my awakening and the birth of my intuition. It required shedding the old ego and feeling fully and unconditionally into my heart and all the emotions that make us human.

Nobody likes to talk about this part. You know, the part where you're no longer a caterpillar but not yet a butterfly. You don't know who you are and you don't know where you're going. You're literally in the dark, confused and uncertain of the future. Some call it a 'Dark Night of the Soul' or the five stages of grief. Whatever you call it, you know that every fibre of your being is calling for transformation. For disruption. For a revolution of the spirit. So surrender. Breakdown the ghastly and make it good again. And then turn the good into gold.

This pose means to me....

Savasana is not the death of you.
It is the dying of who you once were.
This is your rebirth, my love.

There are as many different birth experiences as there are babies. Nobody can predict how a birth will turn out so it is hard to know how to best prepare yourself without having expectations. Ecstatic, sacred, life changing, terrifying, unforgettable, excruciating, shocking, enduring, heartrending, agonising, holy and transformational were words I sometimes heard used to describe childbirth.

I also heard plenty of perfectly natural and smooth birth stories amongst women I knew who barely made it to the hospital on time. Babies born at home, in the car park, in the corridor, basically in transit, between places and spaces. Those babies arrived quickly and drug free. The thing about childbirth, it seemed, was that it was either completely fine or totally fucked up. In control or out of control.

Traumatic was not a word you would typically hear prior to having a baby, in describing childbirth. It was much more likely to spill out afterwards in gory stories and confessional debriefs over a glass of wine with close girlfriends, spoken in hushed comforting tones. Is this in service to our fellow sisters or not? Should we be more open in sharing the emotional experiences that may not be so positive? Our birth 'horror stories' are not told as an exercise in fiction or entertainment. They are told in service because they are the truth and this is a way of healing. Why deny them? We are not spreading our fear, we are meeting our fear - which is far more powerful.

Even though I received all the congratulations when I became a new mother, there was a part of me that was lacking in confidence because I didn't have the experience I had hoped for. I was told that I should feel grateful that my baby was healthy and that should be enough. But it wasn't. That was not ALL that mattered even though 'they' say that. I had compartmentalised the pain and trauma away.

There was a huge hole in the story between me wanting to *give* birth, and someone giving birth *for* me. Doing it incorrectly. I knew intuitively how to make and grow the baby inside of me, so why did I hand over the control when it came to the birth? Instead of me actually giving birth, someone gave birth for me. I submitted to the system and found myself in a cascade of intervention. My power was taken away and put in the hands of the staff in the medical system. My intuition was interrupted. Safety was the driving force behind all the interventions because I was told *what matters most is a healthy mum and a healthy baby*. Of course that was true but surely the health of the mum and the baby also included our emotional, spiritual, psychological and mental health?

Health also means *Wholeness* and a human being is not made up of fragmented bits but is one operating ecosystem connected energetically and psychically to all the elements in nature. Unfortunately because the fear of 'risk' was so strong I didn't trust my own intuition. I didn't speak up and say I wanted to wait until my waters broke naturally. I didn't speak up and say I didn't want to be induced. I didn't ask to have an elective c-section instead. I didn't tell the midwife I wanted more pain relief because I was struggling with excruciating back pain. I was too afraid.

I was vulnerable and in the hands of the professionals. I was relying completely on medical expertise to deliver my baby and the authority of my doctor to make the safest choices. I was relying on him to manage all the risks for the best possible outcome. I was not relying on my intuition at all so I didn't trust my body from the start. I didn't trust my body to give birth, I didn't trust my body to breastfeed and I certainly didn't trust my ability and confidence to raise the baby without a strict controlling routine. I had put all my faith into the medical system to keep me and my baby safe. All my eggs were in one basket.

The two most common birth baskets in our culture are the

midwifery model and the hospital model. One is led by women for women (usually midwives or doulas) and encourages the woman to be at the centre of control. The other is contained within a controlled system with protocols and staffing constraints of which the doctor is at the centre of control. For most of history, an emergency c-section was not intended to save the mother's life, because surgeons did not have the skills to repair a uterine incision without infection. Thankfully in 1882 German obstetrician, Max Sanger, developed sutures that had low rates of infection. He became the father of the modern caesarian. Hospital Chaplain, Karen Hanson, wrote:

"The demise of the midwife started in the nineteenth century as medicine was being drawn into the marketplace and the physician made healing a commodity and a source of wealth in itself."

Surely enough experience has passed now in modern medicine to recognise that women deserve a birth culture that unites the best of both models. There are enough examples of what works and what doesn't. Ideally the model would include the woman's ability to choose exactly how she wants to deliver her own baby as the most important thing.

Perhaps assigning a doula or birth coach for each woman during the delivery would be a better investment in addition to group labour classes. Another woman to be her advocate, to champion her and remind her of her power and her choices when she is in pain and too weak to speak. Wouldn't it be interesting to see if the government ever took on that possibility or would the empowerment of women in childbirth be too frightening to them, or worse still, threaten the financial model? Governments have targets too and the healthcare system is, after all, made up of commercial business.

The pathway most women take is to fit in with the current medical model. A routine practice which is based around fitting birth in limited time frames, around bed availability and staff rosters. Scheduling our doctors, our inductions and our pain relief can all interfere with the natural process. Childbirth for many is a marathon - not a race - and should be an empowering moment of intuitive greatness when you cross the finish line. A celebration and true expression of the feminine form in an environment that supports this safely.

If we could be more active participants, as opposed to passive onlookers sidelined in the endurance race, we would feel a greater sense of achievement. If we could just pause at each drink station, feel the support from the crowd, and pause to re-evaluate each stage then we might know the next best thing to do. If the medical system could take more responsibility for our emotional health as well as our physical safety then the word *traumatic* may be used less to describe the experience. And if we could make our choices without feeling pressured, judged, guilty or rushed then we would trust our intuition. There are a lot of 'ifs' there so I believe beginning the conversation and feeling less afraid to share our stories is a good start to consider freedom of choice as a central theme.

Instead of sitting in awkward silence and taking birth instructions passively as a patient, the code around appropriate 'birth speak' needs a massive overhaul. Not to *play down* the significance of our experiences but actually to *man down*. Birth is not just about making babies. Birth is about making mothers. Strong, feminine, confident, lioness mothers who trust their own roar and fierce decisions.

I wanted my doctor to acknowledge the pain I suffered, the horrendous trauma. The fact that it was the year 2010 and we were not accustomed to such brutal events. I wanted him to perhaps even validate for me that it wasn't a 'normal' thing to go through what I went through. To refer me to a counsellor while the sensation was still raw and I could feel it in my body. Or, perhaps he could even take responsibility for my whole being. That's a wild thought. Can specialists even do that or has the system boxed them into a teeny tiny part of a human? An organ, a bone, a gland, an opening. It's micro-management or macro-medication management. We medicate someone with a heart condition but ignore the fact that it could damage their kidneys. We manage someone's autoimmune disease but ruin their gut lining in the process. We regulate a woman's periods with artificial hormones but render her infertile in the long term. We keep someone alive on medication for years after their mind and spirit has been stolen by the dementia demon. Separation breeds risk.

But whatever is in the micro is in the macro and even though our organs are managed separately in our bodies, the fact remains we are one whole operating system. We are under the influence of the biggest immutable Universal Law of all, 'The Law of Correspondence', which says the outer world is merely a reflection of our inner world.

In humans this applies when we intuitively know that our physical, mental and spiritual health, is all undoubtedly connected. There is no separation since everything in the universe originates from the same 'One Source.' The Ancient Greek Temple of Apollo at Delphi was referring to this great 'Law of Correspondence' in the inscription '*Know thyself and thou shalt know all the mysteries of the gods and the universe.*'

Addiction to numbing substances is always attractive to people who have been through some sort of trauma in their lives or felt victimised. Understandably they don't want to feel the memory of the trauma but the body keeps the score. The memories remain hidden in the cell tissue and it eventually catches up with them. Post Traumatic Stress Disorder (PTSD), post-natal depression and post-natal depletion are therefore more common as a result of the undealt trauma.

My birth story is extreme but it is part of who I am. Understanding it provides the context, the reason and sets the scene for my relationship with persistent pain, medication and the birth of my intuition. I'm not saying there's no place for modern medicine. No doubt, modern medicine needs to jump in and save lives sometimes. It also needs to offer us intervention as an option, but there is lots of room for improvement to consider the *whole* health of a mother in birth. Pain will always be a very natural part of the birthing process but it doesn't have to be if you don't want it to. The mode or orifice of delivery is less important than the fact a woman needs to feel safe, respected and supported.

Women can feel empowered choosing intervention and they can feel victimised during a textbook vaginal birth. The difference is that being empowered means we take an active role rather than a passive role in the process. It should all come down to the woman's individual intuition. What *feels* right for her. What IS empowering. Do you *want* to experience pain or not? Certainly not surgical pain though. I don't imagine any woman *choosing* to feel surgical pain. Unless you are into torture.

'First do no harm' is *not* a choice a doctor gets to make.

To first do no harm is their oath, their promise, their holy orders.

CHAPTER 2

IN BETWEEN BABIES

'Taking time out each day to relax and renew is essential to living well'

I walk in to the kitchen and hand the pee stick over to Mum and simultaneously burst into tears.

"Why do Mums always have to be right," I blurt out, crying ugly tears.

She smiles.

"We just *know*. This is wonderful news!" she says.

"It's too soon, I won't be able to cope, how am I going to do this?" I dissolve into a hot mess on the couch, feeling the full weight of this information. It is too much to bear. I am having another baby, I think to myself as the reality starts to sink in. I'm going to fall off the perch.

I remember when I was ten years old, I once had a yellow pet budgie named Abby who literally fell of her perch and died. I made the fatal decision to put the next door neighbour's male blue budgie, Toby, in the same cage to see if we could breed the two birds. Toby was more than happy to be shacked up with the beautiful golden Abby. So my experiment was successful and make babies, they did!

Abby became a chronic egg layer for the feisty Toby, and one day, after already producing a few rounds of offspring, I noticed she looked really puffy and bloated while she warmed her nest. Later that afternoon I checked on her. There she lay, still and stiff on the bottom of the cage. I realised that day was her last on earth. She was so full of eggs the poor thing imploded. What we females go through to produce children for our partners is felt in every species. I later learnt that the name 'Abby' means '*Father rejoices*'. That would be right.

I know divine intervention works its own schedule. Somehow, deep down, I knew this close succession of babies was meant to be fast for me. A very efficient turnaround of production. Too much time to think about the horrors of the first birth would turn me off the prospect of having any more children. Another baby is going to come while the trauma is still hiding away. I pick up the phone to call my husband.

"I'm so happy! We're having another baby." Father rejoices!

I spend the next few months in anticipation of expanding our family. We make an appointment with our obstetrician and the three of us (Oliver, Leila and I) drive back the now familiar route to his consulting rooms. In an attempt to address the elephant in the room he begins.

"Congratulations! It's great to see you again but I wasn't expecting you back so soon."

I look around his office and feel sick on top of the morning sickness. It is at this moment we have the frank discussion about what happened, what went wrong, and how we can move forward.

"I know I wasn't there for you the first time but I'll make sure that I am this time"' he says carefully.

"You know, you are lucky Leila survived," he says in a hushed tone, leaning back in his chair and eyeing me intently. I wonder if I should be congratulating or high fiving him for his professional opinion like some sort of medical victory has taken place.

"Is all that matters a surviving baby? Even if this means sacrificing my right to bodily autonomy and respect?" I wonder.

"They saved Leila's life, but they never asked me how I felt. The obstetrician and the anaesthetist were also responsible for inflicting horrendous injury on me *and* Leila so what sort of reaction did they expect?" I think.

"This next delivery will be a very controlled pain-free elective caesarian. We will book it in at a different hospital with different staff and ensure it is a smooth procedure," he says. His comments feel rehearsed. Just like that, the decision is made for me.

He moves on quickly, taking my blood pressure and weighing me. He does not ask how I am, perhaps afraid to open up that can of worms. I already assume at this stage that I'm incapable of making the choice of how this next baby will be born.

What I am busting to do is talk about the birth. I want to debrief it, discuss it, dissect and pull it apart and study it like you might a rat in year eleven biology class. No one comes forward to offer an ear or their counsel, perhaps because I appear normal and my baby is healthy.

Although my confidence is shattered, I clear my throat and work up the courage to ask him:

"Can you put me in touch with another mother who has been through a similar experience that I could talk to? It would help to have a conversation with someone who has been through the same thing."

He looks at me blankly for a second.

"No, I can't think of any patients who have been through what you have been through."

***

Leila is now six months old and my belly is clearly pregnant again. My womb rebounds right back to its previous shape making a swollen home for baby number two. When I was first pregnant with Leila, my bump was covered in the latest stretchy sexy mama maternity material. All I want to wear now are my husband's t-shirts. Loose, baggy, faded - exactly like the skin hanging under my eyes.

I'm standing over the stove in the kitchen boiling and mashing vegetables for Leila's now solid diet. The waft of organic mush enters my nostrils and causes me to swallow down vomit and the bitter taste of bile which swells over my tongue. I may as well be adrift on a ship in the middle of the Pacific Ocean. I bob up and down over treacherous waves. I'm constantly seasick and can't get off the damn boat. Leila is all aboard on my hip trying to steer my life and pull my hair into her mouth. Her nappy is full of poo; it mixes with the stench coming from the saucepan. Occasionally in this pregnancy I feel a twinge where my c-section scar is. It reminds me the wound will be open again for business in six months time. A single thin line splitting at the seams as it tries to accommodate the new growth. There is no wind in my sails this time. I rely on the fact there are some oars lying around somewhere.

"Who is the captain of this ship?" I wonder, rhythmically mashing into the saucepan. I want to get off. I want someone to turn this vessel around and drive me right back to harbor. The balance of having a barnacle attached to one side and fishing through the soupy mix of water and vegetables with the other, sets me off into a rocking motion my stomach can't quite sway with. I search for some stability. I decide it is safer on land.

I bundle up the baby and strap her into the pram for some fresh air. Shuffling along the pavement I push purposefully with one hand and clutch a can of diet coke in the other. The only thing which seems to kill the constant sick feeling is this good old corrosive cola. The queasiness subsides momentarily and

I feel a sense of freedom in the sunshine. I walk up to the end of the street, where the path meets the ocean. I turn sharply left and walk beside the beach, feeling the saltwater breeze touching my face. Lightness lifts me up and there is a window of space that brings back the memory of me before I had a child. The daily routine of running through the streets carefree on my own accord was a privilege I took for granted. I decide that this pushing the pram, this liberated feeling, will now be my daily medicine. Before I need to upgrade to a double anyway.

My worries are worn thin by the day of the surgery.

I am scheduled in first on the theatre list, squeezed in before morning tea coffee and cake. The day has been planned and organised for me even before this baby was conceived.

'Next time you will have an elective c-section at 37 weeks'. I swallow hard remembering the message after Leila's birth. This baby's birthday was created before the child even arrived.

I arrive in pre-op and am gowned and waiting for the anaethetist to walk in. I am under someone's control again, stuck to the bed and filled with fear. When he enters he looks familiar. Having worked in the same hospitals we have occasionally passed each other in the corridors but never formally met, I realise. He is neat and well presented with an easy way about him which starts to put my anxiety at ease. He tells me not to worry and reassures me that I will be numb from the waist down but that he won't put me to sleep. I have an opportunity to meet this baby in what is a very carefully edited plan. I am in a calm and present state. I will later learn that my file states I am a 'VIP patient'. I will wonder what sort of special treatment I have received and what the exact criteria is that you need to qualify for this exclusive title. Clearly if you are subject to a big fuck up in the past you get to be treated like a special human the next time you are in hospital. A small price to pay by sacrificing your autonomy and your sanity. Or perhaps it is more like flying first class. The more it costs your overall health, the politer the staff are; addressing you by your full name. I don't get a glass of champagne while I am waiting for take off but I hopefully get some extra mind numbing juice up my IV tube and into my veins. I don't feel more deserving of this VIP experience. If anything, I just wish it to be over as soon as possible.

Oliver is led into theatre and takes position next to me this time so I can see him. As the spinal block goes in I am all head and no legs. There is no feeling beyond the curtain screen in front of my face.

"My feet could be on fire right now and I wouldn't feel it," I think, floating on the bed. I am relaxing into the procedure which surprises me but I'm pretty sure they have added a little gin and tonic into the infusion mix. The mood in the theatre is light and bright. I hear someone turn on music in the background. Nurses are humming and chatting away, asking me if I think I am having a boy or a girl. My obstetrician arrives – it is 9am. He is right on time. He gets to work, with an assistant surgeon by his side. Before I know it I hear a cry, and just like a magician would pull a rabbit out of a hat, hey! Presto! Out pops our new little pet just like that.

It is 9.10am. I know this because the nurse calls out the time.

"Meet your beautiful little daughter," the doctor says as they quickly and carefully wrap her up and bring her over to my face. I completely fall in love. I turn to Ollie.

"This is amazing. I want more, (babies)."

I will later retract this statement but right now, I am heavily under the spell of love and cocktails and magic medicine that means no pain. No pain. I lock eyes with her and spend timeless minutes just staring into her soul. I am unable to break my gaze. I am infused with cosmic wonder.

"Hi Zoe," I greet her. I love this name. It sounds celebratory when you say it. It means '*Life*'. I am so happy she is alive.

As I am taken to recovery, my separation from Zoe hurts. Even though I know she is with her Dad I am much more aware this time that I am not with them. Overnight the discomfort begins to deepen.

A revolving door of staff comes in and out of the room. I am asked over and over again by the nurses,

"Are you in pain?"

There is pain of course, post operatively. The incision throbs and my abdominal wall feels a deep soreness that comes from being spread open by retractors. My intestines have been moved around again which feels really odd. Gas passes through my bowels in new places amongst my organs. It's like everything has to settle into its new internal real estate. I am asked to rate my pain out of ten. The pain I experienced during the first birth had set the bar for my understanding of what a ten should represent. Ten to me implies life-threatening torture and insides being ripped away like you might tear cooked chicken into pieces or pull shredded pork off the bone.

I think hard, not wanting to say the wrong thing.

"It's about a four right now," I say. I try to be as accurate as possible knowing that my pain threshold is a bit skewed and possibly abnormal at baseline.

My answers and her assumptions begin to concern me. They might withhold pain relief from me based on my number out of ten. I feel very vulnerable and small. I am dependent on the care of these strangers to control my most basic right as a patient which is to be comfortable and to not suffer.

"You seem to be managing quite well, why don't we try and see if Zoe is ready to breastfeed? Pop on down to the breastfeeding room. I'm about to start a group class," she says.

I make my way slowly down the hallway wheeling my baby

and hanging onto the trolley like a Zimmer frame. I don't want to disappoint the nurse who is guarding the drugs like a gatekeeper. I enter a smallish room and find a seat among other milking mothers. I smile nervously and am careful not to engage in too much conversation. I don't want to upset anyone or be a difficult patient in case it compromises my access to pain relief.

My breasts ache. They have turned into two hot bowling balls overnight. The skin is marbled with giant blue veins and stretches so taut I think the milk is going to burst through my skin. I sit up and rearrange my baby near my breast. I open my top. I try so hard to breastfeed the baby on the edge of an engorged boulder. She shows absolutely no interest in attaching to a nipple the size of her face. Finally, after my feeble attempts, she manages to latch on and I wince with a pain so sharp it brings tears to my eyes. I look to the doorway and notice a student nurse midwife coming in. She is here to observe my feeble attempts to feed. I keep holding my baby's head and trying my best just willing her to suck but she simply peeps open her little eyes and stares at me as if to say 'What are you doing?' I try tickling her feet to wake her up but that just pisses her off and her face contorts and then converts into an annoyed shriek. You think after childbirth that the pain is over but every new day brings with it a new opportunity to feel harrowing sensations.

Exhausted from all the fussing and manhandling she shuts her eyes and pretends to be back in my womb like a crab seeking safety in its sand hole. The midwife suggests that the student nurse try and express some milk out of my breast.

"This teenage girl is going to milk me?" I think. A sinking realisation kicks in – any remaining scrap of dignity I have left has just gone out the window.

I oblige with the directions thrust upon me. I have failed to breastfeed my own baby and now I am literally in the hands of a trainee farm girl. I don't think she even wants to be in the position of cow squeezer but is merely following her superior's orders. I turn on my best behavior to impress the nurse in charge. I wonder if I am deserving of more pain relief now that I am going along with her plan. Tears spill over my cheeks and pour down my face, dripping off my chin. I look down desperately and silently will Zoe to attach. One of the curious Dads peers his head through the door. I realise a bunch of fathers are hanging around outside waiting for their wives to master the skills of nurturing and sustaining their offspring.

"Your wife's in there crying," I hear him say to my husband. Ollie appears in the doorway and reads the look on my face. This heifer has had it.

Later that same afternoon another nurse appears at my bedside.

"Don't worry yourself about breastfeeding love. She is taking the bottle just fine. With another little one at home you don't need the added stress," she says kindly.

"Bless you," I think. Everything is so intense and full on and it's so reassuring to hear that my mother's instincts are right and that I am not failing at anything.

To this day, I've never forgotten her unexpected words and support. To be validated when you are vulnerable is the highest human act of kindness you can offer a new mother.

***

When I was a child, I decided I wanted to be a mouse breeder when I grew up. I had very high career aspirations to be a vet also, however at eight years old, I was more interested in this particular specialisation.

It all started in grade three when we had a class pet mouse called Ralph. We all took turns taking Ralph outside to play each day. One lunchtime when it was my turn to be responsible for

Ralph, I took him outside and built him a very sophisticated kind of maze out of rocks on the dirt. I then released him and watched him navigate his way through the obstacle course to observe if he would make it to the end point.

Unfortunately, as I stepped over the maze to position myself for a better look at the finishing line I placed my foot down on top of Ralph. Feeling the lump under the sole of my shoe I lifted my foot only to see Ralph flatten and roll onto his back. He had brown fur the same colour as the dirt. He must have been moving so quick I became temporarily blinded as he dashed like the speed of light through his maze. Sadly, that was Ralph's last day on earth.

I remember carrying him in my hands back to the classroom beside myself with grief and shock that I had killed the class pet. My guilt and shame was so overbearing I told my mother that afternoon that we must replace him as quickly as possible. After school she drove me around town to various pet stores on the hunt for rodents that had the exact same fur and beady eyes as little Ralph.

I tried so desperately to replace Ralph and not let the class down, but in the end, my teacher decided we were not going to have another class pet. So I was left with a brand new mouse purchased fresh from 'Animal Land'. My mum felt a bit sorry for me so she agreed that I could keep him which kicked off my home project and early training of becoming a mice breeder. I followed up the first purchase with another in quick succession, and before long was looking proudly at two pairs of beady little eyes exploring their new digs in an aquarium I creatively filled with dirt.

The thing is, you need to be careful when breeding vermin in captivity. As I quickly learnt, it takes mice about three seconds to breed and produce a litter. I remember being shocked one morning to discover when coming down the stairs that the mother had already given birth to her pups. Except something was very wrong. It appeared that their fresh pink skinned bodies were scattered around their terrarium half eaten! They had been cannibalised.

What went wrong? Was this my fault? Which one was the murderer; the mother or the father? This was unpleasant to say the least. After cleaning up the murder scene I rang the vet and enquired about what to do. He said, evidently, every now and then the female mouse eats her young.

If there is no food or water in the tank this can be a reason also apparently, but I quickly assured the vet that I was very diligent in filling up both each day. The other reason, he said, was that the mother intuitively culls her litter down to a size that she can manage if she is under too much stress. If she has too many babies in one go and she can't nurse them all, it is nature's way of ensuring that valuable energy will not be lost on a baby who won't make it. It's part of the natural selection process. The other reason he said, can potentially be because it is her first pregnancy she may not know what to do with the babies. Usually in the wild, there is a more experienced 'midwife mouse' who supports and helps the first timers. A kind of mouse mentor. I know I would have really appreciated a mouse mentor at my home after giving birth.

***

I wake up to one of the babies crying around 5am. Always I wake up to crying. For two years I have woken up to the sound of crying whether that was a baby's whimper or my own. I feel beyond sleep deprived but I know this is the work of a mother so I will not complain. I have started to get into the habit of putting on my active wear as soon as I rise, including my sneakers. I treat motherhood like an extreme sport. Running, wrestling, flying, diving and bungee jumping after two babies physically challenges me so much I may as well apply for Red Bull sponsorship. I am being worn away, becoming leaner and meaner while I intuitively know these two barnacles stuck on my hips are sucking the life out of me.

It is action stations all the way up until 10am and the mummy machine has to keep moving or she won't get everything done. Both babies have already had their morning naps. By this time of day I have cleaned myself, the kitchen, the bottles, the spew stained clothes and the animal litter tray. Even the cat demands more of me these days. Cats are known to be exquisitely intuitive. My cat Missy however, has taken it to a whole other level since I became pregnant a second time. I suppose from her perspective, she was technically the first baby.

I bought her home one day as a kitten to surprise my husband. It didn't go down very well. We kept her all the same though, and she soon became a loving member of our family. The vet told us to buy two of these animals because the Burmese breed especially like company and play well in pairs. We ignored this advice. She was doted upon and received all our attention, so you can imagine how pissed off she was when she realised there were baby humans on the way.

On an emotional level, cats are pretty attuned to our positive and negative moods but they are also connected to the more subtle energetic field which makes them sensitive to intuition. My cat may not be able to talk but she has worked out another way to communicate her dissatisfaction in me and with her new pecking order in the family bloodline.

When I was about eight months pregnant with Zoe I remember packing the hospital bag and getting organised. I laid out all the items on the bed including all the little four zero suits and folded them neatly on top of the bed spread. I went off to do a few things and upon returning discovered a very clear message had been deposited on top of the baby's clothes. Missy very articulately pooed on every item of clothing, one by one leaving a stinking mess on the purest of clean white cotton. She never in her five years of life had missed the litter tray until that day. I got the message loud and clear. She was disgusted and then I was disgusted. The name Missy means *'Bee'* in Greek. She certainly left her sting behind.

I try to get out the door, tripping over the cat in the process, to greet another Groundhog Day with whatever positivity is remaining. It's 10am but I wish it was Happy Hour. By this stage I am dressed, the babies are dressed and I am up to the final preparation of the pram before embarking on a routine coffee excursion. This involves the loading of bottles, nappies, snacks, blah, blah, blah - it's the same every day. Except today something different is happening. I can't seem to push the double pram.

"That's strange," I think to myself as I bend down to check the wheels and make sure nothing is caught in them. The brakes are not on either. I try with all my might to give it another push but it won't budge. The girls' eyes both peer up at me as they turn their little heads around to look at my determined face. They are wondering in their minds why aren't we moving mum?

"C'mon Pram Pusher, get a move on we wanna get out," I read their minds.

I stand at my front door behind my cargo of life and I am unable to move it forward. It is in this moment I have a startling realisation that the engine has stalled. I have run out of fuel and I am just standing there blocking the corridor and holding up the daily schedule. Then it dawns on me.

"The engine of the pram is me! I have no strength left to push. I had no strength to push Leila out of my vagina and now I have no strength to push her out the door. What is wrong with me? Surely this is a faulty start."

I try again with the pushing but can't seem to get the urge. I am exhausted and have run out of all motivation. I need a break, a day off but my babies need me. Motherhood is every day, 24/7. It's become pretty obvious now that I'm overdue for a service. For two years every single morning I have pushed this pram out the front door and now the engine is baked. I look around the vehicle to turn on my hazard lights as this is an urgent situation. My liberating pram has turned on me, on us. It's turned into a liability. So, I do the only thing I can do, the next best thing to a service. I reach for my mobile to call for a lifeline.

"I can't do this anymore," I think. Even my breath is thin and weak. I dial a phone number. My manager answers.

"I think it's time I return to work."

Bananasana

Bananasana Pose

Yin Yoga is rooted in the ancient shamanic tradition of China and in the Taoist philosophy of being at one with everything and in harmony with your own nature. The life force known as 'Chi' is the subtle yet very potent energy that informs nature. Yin Yoga embodies the five elemental energies of Earth, Metal, Water, Wood and Fire. Each represent the qualities of stillness, hardness, fluidity, springiness and lightness. The intention being that the essence of the elements is embodied energetically in the shape.

This pose means to me....

We create more space inside for new life to grow.

Giving birth should be the most natural human function so it disappointed me that my experiences were so clinical. The thing is, I did not have the natural births I dreamt of. I wanted that moment of '*I did it*' as the heroic warrior woman holding her baby up to the sky in victory like Simba in the Lion King. I wanted to *own it*. The birth plan of being hypno-happy in a dark room inside a warm bath with essential oils, massage, mantras and a soft voiced doula was just a fantasy. My first experience was a series of clinical interventions in an under-staffed and over-lit hospital filled with strangers staring at me under some very bright lights. The trainee student doctors stood by witnessing human error and taking notes on what *not* to do. The scent of birth was mixed with the potential of death.

My memory of the event was constantly triggered by this mistake because of an ugly chunky keloid scar across my abdomen that looked like a sword gash. My second birth fixed this scar right up. The doctor cut it out and stitched me up so seamlessly that today if you were looking at me, you can barely notice the scar. He erased it cosmetically just like the 'knifing' never happened. He made the ghastly good again on the outside but it remained an open oozing gash on the inside.

What women wish for during labour is to feel safe, supported and respected. If this is denied, silenced or ignored surely we have just marked the most miraculous empowering moment of a woman's life as an insignificant spectacle.

One man who understood this was a Melbourne obstetrician named Dr Percy Rogers. Dr Percy was responsible for introducing 'Psychoprophylaxis', or the Lamaze technique which was popularised in the 1940s by the French obstetrician Dr Fernand Lamaze.

He writes in his book *Active Labour....*

'In the 1960s fathers were still not welcome in the birthing suite so Percy took it upon himself to collaborate and educate women so that they could

empower themselves with the breathing techniques and other supported methods. The general mood at the time among pregnant women was a rejection of medical intervention during labour. Percy did his own research and studies of cases on deliveries and outcomes of his techniques. Included in his data was the importance of finding out how women felt during childbirth. He actually got all 120 of his own cases to write down their experiences as soon as possible after giving birth. His article was written up and presented in 1967 at the World Congress of Gynacology and Obstetrics.'

Across all parameters in the comparison Percy reported the following...

"... results showed a clear advantage for women being trained. The length of both the first and second stages of labour was reduced; the amount of medication used for pain was hugely lessened; and episiotomies decreased in number, likewise the number of caesarean sections."

He continued to train and educate pregnant women and began to collaborate with other allied health, but he came up against major obstacles.

'Obstetrics was a conservative male-dominated branch of medicine...'

Dr Percy's encouragement for natural birthing and less intervention was causing hospitals to lose customers. The general mood amongst women at this time was a rise in feminism and the power to choose.

'By the mid 1970s, the Royal Women's Hospital (RWH) in Melbourne was so concerned about decline in maternity patients that they invited GPs to join the staff and bring along their midwifery patients. In the late 1970s a Birth and Being Conference held in Melbourne was responsible for the new

Family Birth Centre (FBC) at the RWH. The FBC allowed women to labour with the support of their families in a homely atmosphere, where medical intervention was not allowed, but where medical help was close at hand if required. The centre was part of the hospital, but it functioned independently.'

While midwives are competent and careful, things can go very wrong very quickly during childbirth so emergency back up is always wise. It also formed a Friends of the FBC support group which would be there to follow up women after the actual birth and create a community of connecting parents. It was a success and since has been shared widely around the world as best practice. Sadly, the Melbourne hospital that put in place the first Family Birth Centre in Australia has now eliminated it during a subsequent refurbishment.

It is not surprising that the natural childbirth movement sprung up when it did in the 70s. Women wanted the rights to their choices and to feel empowered during this era of birth control and liberation. Getting caught up in the idealisation of birth is not foolish, it is natural. There is just so much more intervention today than there was fifty years ago. With the accessibility of IVF, the average age of women having babies increasing, and even conceiving a baby in a variety of modern family structures, anything is possible. We have a whole buffet of choices to select from. It's about being educated and informed of what each dish contains and if it is right for you. You don't need to simply eat what is put in front of you. You can get up from your seat and walk around and take a good look at what will nourish you and listen to what your intuition is telling you.

History can teach us a lot. Fanny Burney was a novelist who underwent a mastectomy in her home without anaesthetic in the year 1811. A glass of wine was the only pain relief given to her before they lopped off her right breast. I would have done anything for a taste of chardonnay or maybe a nice french chablis before my first birth but alas, hospitals do not offer such hospitality.

Fanny wrote:

"I began a scream that lasted un-intermittingly during the whole time of the incision – and I almost marvel that it rings in my ears still!"

She was surrounded by seven men in black restraining her as one surgeon controlled the event. Fanny bravely rechanneled her fear into her writing and thereby defused the framework of dominance and submission which she found as oppressive as the physical pain. She lived for another twenty-nine years and it was impossible to tell if her tumor was malignant. What I understand from her story is that she was one strong woman who took her life back into her own hands and re-wrote her medical history from a position of power.

CHAPTER 3

BACK TO WORK

'You are the sky, everything else is just the weather'

After having twenty-four months of maternity leave, I return to my career as a clinical specialist for a medical device company. Life is in full swing. I am exactly like most women I know; doing the juggle and trying to manage a family and employer's expectations whilst also absorbing the mental load of domestic duties. I am enjoying the break from the grind of toddlers and baby life and am *really* enjoying some brain stimulation again.

I meet with patients at clinics in hospitals and in private waiting rooms just like I had before but something this time feels different. I notice changes in the patients I never would have previously picked up on before having kids. I sense some of these people with sick hearts are more depressed or anxious. I observe their nervous energy while they are waiting to get their pacemaker checked. It feels palpable. I detect their vulnerability while I control how fast and how slow their heart beats as I service their pacemaker device.

I feel them hold their breath, shake and stop talking during this check up as they trust me to take their life in my hands for ten minutes. I notice their carer sitting beside them; a loving husband, daughter or friend, holding their hand and saying comforting words to take their mind off their obvious discomfort. I feel a sickening feeling in the pit of my belly when I notice a patient's battery is ready to be swapped and I have to deliver the news that they need to go into surgery as soon as possible. Their only choice to fully trust their doctor and the hospital system as they are committed to a lifetime of surgeries due to the reliance on their implant. I feel at odds knowing that some patients in the public system are fitted with an inferior device with less battery power because they can't afford private health insurance. Public hospitals have budgets like any other business so they can only purchase a certain number of devices each year. This means if you do not have private health cover, you are reliant on a system that requires you to go on a waitlist and then receive a technology that is inferior to what private patients receive. Everything is different yet the people are the same. I am operating humans not machines.

Within the first few months of being back at work, I'm called to a case at the local children's hospital. When babies are born with congenital heart block they need a pacemaker implanted for their survival. After changing my clothes, throwing scrubs on in a hurry and organising the stock I need, I peer through the window into the theatre. I'm fixing my face mask and tying it into the back of my head when I notice the patient on the table. The patient is only about 40cm long and has hands the size of two twenty cent pieces. The humidicrib is parked outside the giant swinging doors and a soft pink blanket covered in flowers rests inside. The patient is a little baby girl.

I enter the sterile space which buzzes and blinks with technology. The surgeon is preparing the tray and counting instruments with his assistant and scrub nurse. Everything has to be counted for. Swabs, scalpels, catheters, emotions, control, control, control. I find my place in the corner and set my equipment up methodically, checking everything twice over. There is no room for error. I examine the patient file and start to take notes on my paperwork.

'Lucy Walker,' Born – 3 weeks ago.

I look up at the table and see she is draped exposing only a few square inches of skin on her torso. She looks like a doll, almost plastic-like. The ventilator breathes for her like two mini mechanical air bags that move her chest rhythmically up and down. The anaesthetist keeps a watch on her vital signs and works with joyful child-like humour. With the wires in place and successfully attached to her heart, I hand over the device ready for connection. The size of the pacemaker takes up most of the surface area in her abdomen. The surgeon creates a pocket and fills her insides with metal. It starts pacing immediately and up on the screen I look in awe as the machine becomes human. With this success, the mood in the room becomes light and I feel a certain level of sacred 'love in action' as the reverence for a young life is celebrated. Babies are born vulnerable and treated in hospitals with a different degree of humanity. I ponder how the patient is viewed as God in this room, the surgeon is the servant.

The following morning, I pull up at a local private hospital early after dropping the girls at daycare. I have been called in to theatre for an emergency implant case for a cardiac arrest patient. I'm in a rush and walk quickly and with purpose towards the hospital entrance until something stops me dead in my tracks. It's him. The doctor that delivered Leila. The last time I saw his face was in theatre on the other side of the curtain screen. He is kind of hanging around the side of the building looking down at his phone. His fingers are moving swiftly over his device as he looks up at me. I see those squinty eyes again. They still appear bloodshot. It transports me immediately back to a memory I'm not sure how to process. All I know is that my breath is fast and I am physically shaking at being so unexpectedly confronted by the sight of him. I recognise his facial expression and it doesn't change as he sees me in front of him. I feel sick when I realise he doesn't know who I am. He can't even remember me as a patient, as a person. He stares blankly at me and moves aside to clear the path for me and allow me and my giant suitcase filled with stock to walk past.

"Sorry," he mutters, shuffling out of the way. Not the apology I was hoping for.

Hospitals are like rabbit warrens; mazes of winding corridors, hidden staircases and grim floors. They are buildings piled upon buildings piled upon buildings like a game of Minecraft. I make it to the clunky lift and squeeze myself into the tight space. It lacks oxygen and light. My chest heaves as I try to breathe quietly to hide the fact that I am freaking out inside from the other people in the lift. My stomach falls to my knees and I fight back tears. I feel dizzy and terrified. I try to focus on watching the floor level numbers going up to avoid eye contact with anyone and avoid passing out. The doors slide open and I practically fall out and find myself in the middle of the Angiography Lab where the patient is already draped and lying on the table being prepped like a millet mignon steak in a French kitchen. I can't tell if it is male or female. The rush and pressure of getting here in time shifts me into work mode and I robotically go about assessing the situation. The staff are hygienically and meticulously proceeding with the order of service and theatre protocol. There is a quiet and efficient busyness about the way they work. I glance at the doctor, who is staring wide-eyed at an image of this patient's heart on the screen. He motions excitedly for me to come over and take a look. It's not often I see this level of enthusiasm on this doctor's face so I am curious as what is sparking his interest.

"Come and look at this rare picture," he says. As a patient, you never want to hear the words *Rare* and *emergency* in combination. *Routine* and *common* are much safer. I take a look at the screen and notice a really enlarged heart that is ballooning in a wave like motion.

"The patient has Takotsubo Cardiomyopathy. The left ventricle has stopped beating and is bulging like a giant jellyfish. They call it Broken Heart Syndrome. It gets its name from a Tako-tsubo which resembles something a Japanese fisherman uses to trap octopuses," he says. I start to wonder about the person under the drapes. I check the patient sticker to see the name. Wanda Brown, a fifty-six year old woman.

"What causes it?" I ask.

"Well, it's a case of stress and shock. Usually some sort of severe emotional trauma such as grief, loss of a family member or an accident maybe. There is a surge of stress hormones adrenalin, noradrenalin and cortisol that basically floods the chambers making it unable to contract to the point it can't function normally. We'll try and medically manage her first and then we'll put in a defib. Her EF is low and her QRS is wide too," he says matter-of-factly.

I wonder what broke this woman's heart. The stress hormones and shock are her response to her own fear and emotional pain. The human heart is so much more than an organ and a pump. How do we treat the entire human here? As I observe her ECG and vital signs the other half of me wants to connect, talk to her, hold her hand and tell her she is not alone.

The case progresses like clockwork and a short time later the implant is installed, now part of this woman's anatomy. While the surgeon is sewing the patient up I begin to finalise my paperwork and am distracted by a text message on my phone.

It reads: *'URGENT - While you are there, can you please do a device check on deceased Mrs X in the morgue for Dr XYZ'.*

As the final dressing is applied to Wanda I'm packing up my gear and getting ready to move on to the next job. It's not uncommon to always move quickly with a sense of urgency.

Not just because it's a medical emergency, but also because I feel uncomfortable keeping patients waiting too long. Even though the next patient is clearly in no rush, I find myself still moving like I'm running out of time. Being back at work I'm busy constantly but not in a way most people understand. I'm busy taking deeper breaths. I'm busy silencing irrational thoughts. I'm busy calming a racing heart. I'm busy telling myself I'm ok. I'm busy trying not to think of being late to pick up my kids from daycare. I'm busy pretending to have a smile on my face. It's exhausting.

Making my way back to the lift dragging my suitcase of stock behind me, I wait for the doors to open and wedge myself between the back wall and a gurney. I reach over and press the letter 'B' for Basement. I wonder why morgues are always in the basement of a hospital. Is it supposed to be symbolic of dead bodies under the ground? I inappropriately laugh out loud when I think of the way we used to answer the landline at home. 'Hello, city morgue you stab 'em we slab 'em'. Blackness and basements can be funny when we want them to be. As the lift hits the ground I put on my serious but professional face. The word 'morgue' is actually French and means *'to look at solemnly'*. I prefer the term 'Rainbows End' we sometimes use when having conversations in front of patients or children.

The chilled air hits me straight away and the goose bumps prickle the hairs on the back of my neck exactly as if I have been spooked. I press the buzzer to the security door and wait for the coroner to give me access. As I'm directed to the patient I'm looking down at my phone for my directions.

'Can you turn OFF detections and print out an event summary of episodes.'

Determining the cause of death for a patient can be a turning moment for any family. Did she die naturally? Was she in pain? Was it quick? What was she doing right before she died? The technology holding all the secrets of this person's activity is still alive, still recording. I take a deep breath and walk over to the holding bay where she is waiting for the funeral home to come and collect her. As I set up my machine my stomach makes some really loud grumbling noises because the afternoon has passed me by without lunch. I place my programmer head over her chest. Her face is covered but I sense this person had her own children. I sense she is a grandmother. I sense she is a wise woman. As I'm reaching over her body my thigh brushes up against something tickling me. I look down and notice her black fingernails curled up against my pants. My stomach does a backflip and I hide her arm back underneath the crisp white sheet. The device starts to download all the information and long sheets of paper are printed out onto the hard floor around my ankles. I look down at the typing and notice today's date. It's 6 May 2013. The same day my father died six short years ago.

Shoelace
Pose

Shoelace Pose

We are humans not machines. I don't believe the body is a combination of parts like a machine. I believe in the Tao in terms of wholeness that there is no one part of the body that is separate from everything else. Your mind, body, spirit and soul is all connected. This Yoga pose is about feeling everything and not fragmenting yourself into bits. The Tao means 'the way' – that is the way of nature.

This pose means to me...

Even when we tie ourselves into a knot freedom follows.
We find expansion inside contraction.
Light in the dark.
Love in fear.

Caroline Myss states in her book *Anatomy of the Spirit*:

'Life crises that have issues of love at their core – divorce, death of a loved one, emotional abuse, abandonment, adultery – are often the cause of an illness. Physical healing often requires, and may demand, the healing of emotional issues....whereas disease was once thought of as caused by essentially lower chakra sources – genetics and germs – we now view the origin of disease as stemming from toxic emotional stress levels.... Our entire medical model is being reshaped around the power of the heart.'

Medical training demands a kind of disembodiment by doctors. I know from experience that 'emergencies gone wrong' are used later on as case studies for medical trainees learning *what not to do*. Patients are vulnerable and are always used as opportunities to learn and to train on in the system. I wonder about the complexity of the medical system and the lack of human connection in follow up. How did the doctor who delivered Leila feel being responsible for the outcome? I guess it serves him to be detached. I don't know this for sure because I never had the chance to have a conversation with him let alone receive a visit from him after the birth. Our doctor-patient relationship dissolved immediately after the baby was rescued.

Medicine doesn't pause to acknowledge trauma and assess the emotional wellbeing of its patients, let alone indulge them in that awareness. Doctors are not trained on what to do with shame. In our modern society fear may force them to practice a kind of defensive medicine. Obsessed with the paranoia that they might be sued if they don't intervene. Fear can influence decisions and choices that support *control* rather than *intuition*. The greater the risk, the greater the chance the system will attempt to control outcomes. This emphasis around risk reduction shifts the decision making from what might be the right thing for the patient, to what might be the right thing for the institution.

Doctors are humans after all and make mistakes all the time. It is these errors in judgement which expose their own vulnerability.

After Leila's birth I did receive an apology. But it wasn't from a person. It was a carefully worded letter from the hospital, clearly on advice from their legal department. An official apology containing a couple of paragraphs on one sheet of paper. There were some friends and family who suggested getting a lawyer involved to sue for medical negligence and receive some kind of compensation. This was an option however one that would involve money, time and energy - all of which I had none, being pregnant for the second time and looking after a baby. The letter had no positive effect on my wellbeing and quickly joined the pile of bills on the kitchen counter. The compensation I was seeking was to simply be treated like a human, not a liability.

CHAPTER 4

SILENCE

'The quieter you become, the more you are able to hear'

There was a time before my career when my experience of the medical system highlighted the mystery between pain and beauty and the great polarity that exists between suffering and love. The day my father died was a moment in history that opened me up to this idea that death is a natural part of life. It shouldn't take place in an unnatural environment, but it so often does. Death is so certain to us all but somehow we are still surprised by it.

Paradoxically Dad's death occurred during a weekend celebration of love. My wedding. He didn't make it to the ceremony even though I knew how excited he was to wear his new hot pink tie for the event. He picked it out especially because he liked to wear crazy colourful clothing. The brighter the better. I think he also chose it because he was sending off his little girl, me. His gift to me that weekend was the wedding song he picked out - 'Always Look on the Bright Side of Life'. He was planning to sing it to us, so in his absence, the whole party joined in chorus and belted it out together. His presence was felt by all.

Our wedding was a fantastic memorable event filled with bright moments and it wasn't until the following day that we received the call. It was our post wedding recovery day and we were consuming wedding cake and cocktails in the backyard of a fabulous beach house in Byron Bay. I'm pretty sure Ollie had just opened the tequila and was sharing shots with his friends when my sister came over.

"It's time to go," she said. I knew exactly what she meant and my heart sank.

"Now? The party is just getting started." My father never did like to miss out on a good party. Ollie and I climbed into the backseat of the car - it wasn't really the newlywed send off we had in mind. There were no empty cans or decorative paraphernalia hanging off the boot. Just a husband and his new wife going to say goodbye to her father.

Dad had a very medicalised death in palliative care controlled by doctors in hospital. I remember noticing the absence of anything sacred which I felt like the moment deserved. My father was an artist, an eccentric character who embraced his creativity through his art. He was fortunate to be able to do his soul's work. He loved nature, music, drawing, painting, sculpting and making things and wanted to reincarnate into his next life as his spirit animal 'the eagle'. The name Eugene means *'well born'* so I knew he would have no problem with a rebirth if he was to live up to his name.

However, I didn't feel like his end of life was preparing him properly for this transition. Where was the clear blue open sky, the fresh air and the wonderous mountain ranges that eagles soar around? At least hang some inspiring artwork and photography on the walls. Why is colour therapy so liberally applied in children's hospitals but denied for the dying? Instead, palliative care was a dull and bland place with each death room the same carbon copy of one another. I know it's not where I would want to leave my body. Put me somewhere on a beautiful beach next to a bonfire under the full moon with a bunch of yogis and mystics 'Omm-ing' over me. I want to be surrounded by friends and family and children and animals. Not stuck in a hospital bed hanging on every word the doctor says.

"Won't be long now, kidneys have shut down, everyone line up and visit between 2pm and 4pm to say your goodbyes." No thanks. Most people would not consider that an ideal death. Have we outsourced dying to medicine?

I wanted to ease his pain and his struggle to breathe. The disease had taken his physical body aggressively and I needed to know he was ok inside. Even though he couldn't speak or show any signs of consciousness there was a part of him I needed to connect to. A natural death from cancer looks completely unnatural. My Dad was never a big man but cancer made him tiny. He shrunk so much his skin hung off his bones and he turned grey all over. The slowness and effort to take a single breath was like torture to witness. As his body shrunk closer to the end his spirit grew until the room became thicker with it.

I approached a nurse.

"I feel so helpless I don't know what to do," I said.

This woman looked at me.

"Why don't you pray?"

"But I don't believe in God," I replied. What she said next has always stayed with me:

"God is not something you believe in, God is an experience."

***

It is my Father's last day on earth so I go to his bedside and hold his hand.

I am not a newlywed in my late twenties when I sit next to my dying Dad.

I am six years old again and sitting in the wheelbarrow as he drives me around the backyard.

I am ten sitting in the back of his truck making countless trips to the dump with my head sticking out the car window like a happy dog.

I am thirteen tentatively listening to him on the phone tell my music teacher that I want to 'break up' with piano lessons.

I am twenty-eight and somehow he knows that I have just married the love of my life and it is time for him to pass the baton to another man. He knows I will be looked after. He knows it is safe to go now.

I intuitively sense his spirit going as I hold his hand and close my eyes. Silence surrounds our skin. There is an exchange between us which is beyond my five senses and I feel at peace at last knowing his physical suffering is almost over.

Years later, I will close my eyes and remember this day and still feel the warm sensation of his hand wrapped around mine. I will know it's not physically there but it won't matter because beyond my five senses it will be. It is greatly comforting and takes away the feeling of grief and loss.

"This must be the experience of God," I think to myself. I get up and leave the hospital; in that moment deciding it's time to go before I see him take his last breath. I know he is already gone. Later, I will be told that some people were surprised at this decision as they watched the back of me leaving the building on the way back to my honeymoon. One hour after leaving the hospital I receive the call that he has passed.

Attending his funeral for me was a joyful occasion. I know some people may not understand this but I did not shed one tear at my father's service. I felt like he had taken flight and I was so happy for him that he was free of his body.

Poem I read at my father's funeral

'The Eagle' by Emily M. Parris

The eagle is a magnificent bird
Who soars with graceful ease
He's a symbol of our heritage
As he glides upon the breeze

He's a symbol of our freedom
In his soaring boundless flight
A beacon for humanity
And a splendid, noble sight

His huge wingspan maneuvers him
In boundless soaring flight
Oh eagle, in your majesty
May we follow you tonight

May we soar like eagles on the wings
Of dreams composed of light
Oh, eagle, in your splendor
May we follow you tonight

It takes reflecting on my dad's death to understand how vulnerable we all are and how reliant we have become on the medical system for birth as well as death. We depend on the skills of the carers but also the compassion and human right for pain management, dignity and respect.

We begin and we end in the same way.

Tina Bruce

Melting Heart
Pose

Melting Heart Pose

In Yin Yoga the posture is the least important part of the practice. Rather it is about removing the blocks so that your spirit can flow and your intuition can land again in your heart.

This pose means to me....

The beginning of learning to be vulnerable.
Opening the heart space towards
the mother earth is the first offering.

As the Heart Coherence Method by the *Heartmath Institute* teaches us, the heart is a thinking and feeling organ. It contains Neurocardiocytes, around 40,000 to be precise, which is *a lot* of feelings in our heart chakra field. To be a healthy human and move from a fear state towards the vibration of love, feeling these emotions is essential to becoming whole. Depending on how skillful we are at hiding or suppressing stress, our very survival may depend on us doing this *heart work*. We may need to relearn what is at the very core of our own innate nature. We are born with intuitive hearts but over time, they become covered up with layers of our own fear.

When we were in the womb, we were nurtured by the sound of our mother's heartbeat and its 'lub-dub' rhythm. It was soothing and essential for our brain development as babies. So my understanding is that our intuitive intelligence requires both the giving and receiving of our emotions. We need to feel it flow *both* ways and learn not to suppress it even when it's uncomfortable or painful. On that level it represents our right as a human being to love and be loved in return. I feel like I am still learning its language because as attractive as it is, it is in equal parts, intimidating.

While practicing my own *heart work*, I observed two types of energy systems at work. One which we can measure electrically with physical equipment such as ECG monitors, and one which we cannot, being the subtle energetic anatomy or chakra system. The heart is our fourth chakra and is the central powerhouse of the body which is the bridge between the lower three and upper three chakras. It is our mission control centre. It houses all our emotional energy designed to express compassion, courage, forgiveness and love.

In my experience, I believe these two energy systems are directly related. The very first mathematical equation you learn as a 'Heart Sparkie' is *Ohm's Law.*

Which is...

Voltage = Impedence x Resistance

The fundamental relationship found in electronic circuits. In other words, if you increase the Voltage through a circuit whose Resistance is fixed, the Current (or energy) goes up and you gain power. Likewise, if you block or increase the resistance, you lose power.

So, coming back to our lady with Takotsubo, if we apply it emotionally through the *Law of Heart Coherence* (I just made that up) it looks like this...

Pain x Resistance = Suffering

The more we ignore, numb or resist our own pain, the more power we lose and the greater we suffer. To keep fear and pain contained inside the heart is *hard work* and it requires *heart work* to get it out. To finally free fear from the prison of the pericardium walls. Many people keep the doorway to their heart firmly shut. This is often obvious with their posture and body language. Rounded shoulders and a kyphosis in the upper back develops as they try to protect the chest area from being open and vulnerable. Years of repressed raw emotional data and wounded childhood memories can stay contained in that space and eventually lead to dis-ease, perhaps even from generations prior to our existence.

The questions contained within the fourth chakra will be presented to you again and again in your lifetime, until the answer eventually breaks your heart. But it doesn't have to be that way if you choose to do the *heart work* and practice connecting to this place every day. Remember, the purpose of our heart is to love. So loving ourselves in the form of self compassion is the essential key to finding fulfillment that we are often convinced lies outside of ourselves. Finding distractions and comfort in the form of food, alcohol, work, shopping and relationships is all part of the human experience. Which is why we don't easily pursue these questions of self-exploration because we know, deep down, the answers will require us to change our lives. This path through the heart is the truth and it is non-negotiable no matter what spiritual tradition one chooses. Your love is wise and wants to be revealed. Place your hand over your heart, close your eyes, and feel love. The silence is golden.

CHAPTER 5

THIS IS GOING TO HURT

*'A cup of tea
is like having a bath
on the inside'*

I am on my way home from work. I am going as fast as I can to pick up the kids from childcare on time. Any mother who works and juggles multiple children is most certainly trying to do her best. Finishing up a work call and rounding off the conversation for the fifth time in the car, I run into the childcare centre to deal with domestic matters. I can feel a kind of pressure beneath the surface of my skin to move with urgency. Switching my attention instantly from sales reports to kid reports as I step through the gate, I am faced by staff with their daily download.

'Zoe refused to eat her tomatoes again,'

'Leila didn't share her toys with Tommy',

'Zoe walked away from the magic circle',

'Leila wet her pants but then proceeded to do a poo on the potty!'

All I need is bullet point information so I can scrounge up my dirty paint stained children and convince them I have jelly beans in the car. I'm not up for a chat. Please give me your elevator pitch so I can get the hell home and start dinner!

Leaving the building, I begin the toddler to vehicle loading process from sidewalk to car door while vigilantly restraining them from running straight into traffic. Click clack, I secure one child and walk around to the opposite side to secure the second. As Leila climbs into her seat I hastily hurry her in, not realising her little hand is still holding on to the spot between the hinge and the car door.

I begin to close the door to signal her to hurry and hear a horrible sound. My gut response alerts me to an interior biological crunch. The realisation hits that I may have just crushed my daughter's hand in the car door and it feels like a blow to the stomach. A millisecond later a blood curdling scream confirms my worse fears. Yep, those were bones that I heard. Her pain then becomes my pain, a thousand times over.

As I search for the damage I am expecting to see a hand without fingers attached, however, they are luckily all still there, albeit mangled. I drive back to the Emergency Department for the second time that day. Weaving through peak hour traffic as she screams in the back seat, my nervous system is now at gunpoint.

I arrive at the hospital with my casualty and pass her over to the system. We take a number and wait to be called. The triage nurse takes us in for an assessment and for a moment gives me a careful look up and down as she asks Leila exactly how it happened.

"Mummy closed the door on my hand," she says innocently.

"Oh dear, that must have really hurt," the nurse replies. She looks at me again but no words are spoken or reassurance offered. I swallow the lump of guilt in my throat. After five hours of waiting, x-rays and examinations I can breathe a small sigh of relief that the damage is minimal. Leila is fortunate that her hand is still so small that the tiny bones are really flexible and bent with the hinge. No breaks. Her three fingers almost severed the skin at the base of the joint but just need a couple of stitches. She happily watches Peppa Pig in the hospital while I am left traumatised by the accident, knowing intuitively I could have avoided it if I'd slowed down enough to listen to the voice inside me. *Don't rush, take your time, all will get done.* My body is still shaking as I load her back into the car to go home.

***

Slamming Leila's hand in the door was only the first time this type of shared shock vibrated through me like an earthquake, unfortunately. Following this event there was the time Leila yanked her sister's arm playfully and dislocated her elbow. Witnessing Zoe's arm bone being put back in its socket was similar to an electricity jolt shooting through my veins like lightening. Then there was the day Leila landed on her sister's arm and this time broke both Zoe's wrist bones. I had to drive to the children's hospital on the rainiest day on record in Melbourne since 1936 while she howled blue murder so loudly it quaked right through my skin from the backseat. The trauma of her scream, visceral in its pitch, quivered my internal organs and pushed my heart up into my throat. There is no 'mothering' or comforting you can do when your hands are tied to the steering wheel. You become the shock absorber inside the vehicle. Your role to be the driver and sounding board for the audible notes of pain to play a song all over your soul. 'Keep your eyes on the road', was all I could say in my mind. Noticing that the traffic light was actually green.

"I'm sure that is the sign to go forward," I thought.

"Light is green," I repeated out loud, just to understand my own intention to stay safe while feeling totally incompetent to operate such a heavy machine.

Then there was the time Leila swung off the monkey bars practicing the 'death drop' after school and landed on her left hand instead of both feet. By this stage I was deeply familiar with what a 'broken' cry sounded like. I could tune it like a fine instrument. Within five minutes I intuitively knew I was feeling a fracture. Her crying, her shaking, her shivering all transferring onto me, reminding my nervous system that it knows what to do with this information. Fight it, flee it or freezing it were my options. I went with freezing it that day.

"Why don't we just sleep on it and see how it is in the morning?" I suggested. Some Panadol, a bandage and an ice cream later and we were good weren't we? But I knew better. I was just waiting for my nervous system to catch up because I was more traumatised than she was!

I didn't need x-rays to know this but complied with the system anyhow. Off we headed on yet another journey to the children's hospital. Emergency wait rooms are such tense environments filled with uncertainty and suffering. As I looked around at the familiar walls I admired the artwork and colours printed on the curtains. We were approached by two volunteers dressed up as Superwoman heroes. Their role was to wander around and entertain sick children waiting to be seen by a doctor. They pulled games and toys out of their magic backpack creating smiles and a little relief for the parents. While I sat there grateful for the first happy face I had seen on Leila all day, I then found myself joining in and playing a card game of Uno. Leila laughed as they made fart jokes every time they moved the chair closer. Humour has such an amazing affect on people's energy. It's designed to raise spirits and I wondered why it all stops once you reach adulthood. Our pain levels don't stop so why do we get treated differently when we grow up? The more mature we are, the more trauma baggage we collect but the bleaker and more depressing hospitals become. It makes no sense. The medical system need the comedians, not the pubs and clubs. My inner child responded to the magic and for a moment the tension and stress evaporated.

As the triage nurse assessed the damage she asked Leila, "Have you had any Panadol or Nurofen?"

"No not today," I replied for her.

"It's very swollen," the nurse said. "Why haven't you given her anything?"

Then she looked directly at Leila and said, "You know Leila, you are allowed to ask for pain relief."

(as if the thought to medicate my child had never crossed my mind).

"Another mummy fail," I thought.

***

The dentist is not excluded from this list of shared pain experiences. Like a dog knows its car trip is destined for the vet, Zoe is barking all the way from the back seat as we drive to an appointment to fix her teeth. As we enter the door she is holding onto the back of my shirt filled with trepidation and deep concern around going back to *the chair*. The dentist being a female is bright eyed and wide smiled as she happily chats away to Zoe about school holidays, Alice in Wonderland and our promised trip to the book shop after this appointment is finished. Encouragingly, Zoe starts to relax and I feel comfortable enough to flick through a magazine in the corner enjoying a little moment to myself reading an article.

I hear the metal sounds of scraping tools against her mouth suctioning and swirling through tubes. The expectant smell of sterility and chemicals fills the air and I swallow to soothe my dry throat and the queasiness in my belly. There is a pause in the chit chat for a moment and I hear from the dentist, "Mum, are you aware of the enamel hypoplasia on her back molars?"

"Yes, I reply. "That is why we are here so you can seal them up."

"Ok, it just looks like since you were last here that part of the tooth has decayed and broken off. Unfortunately, these are permanent adult teeth and we will need to fix this problem today."

"She is going to have this condition for the rest of her life. It was caused when she was a developing fetus in utero and something has compromised the matrix formation."

"It's usually a mineral deficiency as a result of the mother taking medication which is passed across the placenta during the exact time these teeth were forming. Were you on antibiotics at all when you were pregnant?" she asks.

"No, not that I remember," I say. I start to rack my brain for all the reasons that I could be the cause of Zoe's sensitive and damaged teeth. She looks at me again, "Are you sure?" she asks carefully.

"Yes, I'm sure," I say. I'm starting to feel like a schoolgirl being scolded.

"Well, you are going to have to be a bit more careful with her sugar intake and watch that you are monitoring her hygiene more closely."

I sink a bit lower into my chair and feel my dry throat becoming lumpier as the guilt rises up all too easily.

The dentist says to Zoe, "I will have to apply these fissures now so I will use my magic sleepy stuff to rub on your cheek and numb the area, is that okay?"

Zoe nods silently and she proceeds with her work.

"There we go, that tooth should be nice and sleepy now so I'm going to start putting on its special Band-Aid," she says. She blows air on top of Zoe's tooth and she flinches and squeals. The cold rush is still too sensitive.

"It hurts," she cries. The dentist reassures her it is just the sound of the tube blowing and tries again. Zoe cries out and this time tries to move her head away. The dentist pauses and considers her options for a moment. She picks up the phone and suddenly an assistant enters the room and stands on the other side of the chair ready for action. Zoe sits up with tears in her eyes now spilling over her cheeks from underneath the pink glasses designed to shield her from the bright lights. She reaches her little hand out to me and is scared.

I immediately walk around and squat on the floor next to the chair so I can hold her hand. The dentist looks at me and says, "I am going to have to give her an anaesthetic which will numb the whole side of her face. It's going to mean she won't feel anything for the next four hours but I need to get in there and fix this."

Zoe is shaking her head now, no way is she going to open her mouth after experiencing the sharpness of nerve pain and the repeated torture this is now creating. The assistant holds her left hand while I hold her right. I use my other arm to rest across her chest.

"Zoe, I am going to try another potion which is much stronger so you don't feel anything. Your face might feel really swollen and your cheek chubby but I promise you it isn't bigger," she says.

Zoe is still shaking her head with her mouth jammed shut so I try and calm her down using my body contact to soothe her. Her arms and legs are tense and she's clenching her fingers around mine. I notice my breath become faster and shallow as my heart pounds in my chest.

"It's ok darling, it will be over really quickly," I lie. My voice shakes but I am trying to be strong. The dentist clamps her mouth open and dives head first down Zoe's throat racing against the clock to finish what she started. Reactively, Zoe immediately tries to jump off the chair and there I am restraining my own daughter, physically holding her down while this professional is inflicting unimaginable trauma onto her without her consent.

Immediately I know she is still experiencing pain even though they gave her the anaesthetic. How is this happening again? A familiar scene takes over my nervous system and there is a wild animal inside of me trying to escape. I'm filled with resistance but know at the same time if Zoe swallows the chemicals the dentist just squeezed into her mouth she will be seriously sick. I can feel Zoe's heart thumping out of her skin like it is trying to escape. For a moment we are in sync sharing this experience together as only a mother and daughter can. The dentist pulls out, sits back and says

"All done sweetie, you were so brave, well done."

I want to throw myself on top of my child and tell her she is safe and I'm so sorry she had to go through that. Zoe sits up confused, her face is bright red, she is balling her eyes out and wondering why it all happened.

"You said it wouldn't hurt Mum," she cries accusingly.

***

My grandmother is someone who lights up when nursing a great-grandchild in her arms and whose presence automatically soothes and nurtures. She is one hundred and one years old at the time I am writing this. A cup of tea with Nan always feels like a warm bath on the inside, and it is during one of these cuppas, holding one of her signature knitted blankets draped over my lap, that I learn more about the woman she was beyond being my maternal grandmother.

She gave birth to five children, her first birth being so traumatic she describes it as the worst moment of her life. In January 1946 she went into labour with her first child in hospital. Back then, childbirth was regarded as "secret women's business" and husbands were not allowed in with the mothers. Rather confusingly, it was also kept a secret from women themselves. The medical staff were the only ones who could comment on how you were to give birth. So Pop was automatically blocked at the door by a nurse and sent home while Nan was ushered into the labour ward in isolation. The nurse would dutifully follow the doctor's 'fad' orders which was to routinely administer pain relief to a woman upon entering whether she needed it or not. Nan spent most of her time labouring on a stretcher by herself close to the ground because there weren't enough beds in the maternity ward. The nurse would pop in and out for routine observations, but support for a first-time mother in hospital was limited.

As she was transitioning in labour, a bossy midwife as stern as an iron rod demanded that Nan be moved up and onto a bed that had just become available. It wasn't the midwife's preference to check the dilation standing as she didn't want to damage her back. Nan did not what to move. She was in 'the zone' and consumed by the urge to push. Her body was instructing her to stay where she was and to start pushing as she could feel the head crowning. She ended up being forced to obey the nurse's orders however and moved up onto the bed. A little baby girl, was born shortly after.

Nan intuitively knew something wasn't quite right with her baby. The midwife who delivered her was acting sheepishly strange after the birth also. She was being overly nice and compensating for something. Nan said she sniffed the guilt all over her and knew that the midwife's decision to move her body at the end stage of labour may have cost her child its life. Her intuition sensed that the real truth was being hidden from her. The following day the baby died of a cerebral intracranial haemorrhage. No one will really know for sure if the cause of death was due to a traumatic birth injury caused by medical negligence during the delivery. But what remains is my Nan's experience and mother's intuition that there was more to the story, and typical of that generation, it was swept under the carpet and remains a mystery.

My Nan wasn't allowed to nurse the baby or hold her after

her death. She said all she saw was the back of her baby's head being carried out of her hospital room by her own mother after she died. Shielding her from the trauma, which actually did the opposite and forever left a gaping hole in her heart. There was no funeral, ceremony or service to say goodbye back in those days. She named her precious first baby Pamela.

"How did you go on after that Nan?" I asked her.

"I fell pregnant again straight away. I think it was a mistake though because we were still too emotional and deep in grief."

The trauma and loss she experienced was quickly diverted with another pregnancy.

Just like me, she gave birth to her second daughter within twelve months. Kathy, my aunt, lived until she was thirty and died the year I was born in 1979. She passed away after a long battle with mental illness choosing to end her own suffering and life. Unfortunately, the doctor caring for Kathy took advantage of her vulnerable and fragile condition and pursued a sexual relationship with her. He abused his power as a psychiatrist manipulating his patient to suit his desires.

The tragedy of losing another child weighing heavily on my Nan's memories. I can't imagine how it would feel for any parent to lose their own child in this way. Over the years she had three more children, including my Mum, and thank goodness she did or I wouldn't be here writing this book.

Her dear beloved husband Bruce passed away in 1993. He went into hospital for a very routine overnight procedure and never came out. He became infected with a hospital acquired infection and died within days from septicemia. The risk of the medical institution claiming another life short of its years.

"Do you still think about all the losses Nan?" I asked her.

"Yes all the time, but you become less sensitive about it as you get older. You learn to take the good with the bad and accept whatever life dishes out to you."

It was wise advice from an independently living one hundred

and one year old wise woman. I understand the *good with the bad* bit, but it was the *accept it* part I struggled with.

"How do you accept the pain and forgive others who have done the wrong thing?" I asked.

"You become bitter or you become benevolent," she replied. I sort of understood that benevolent meant something holy or sacred but I was unsure what the exact definition was so I looked it up.

Benevolent; well meaning and kindly, serving a charitable rather than a profit making purpose, expressing goodwill, helpful and gracious.

It seemed being of service to others is what pulls you through such shitty circumstances. Nan poured most of her energy into charity, in particular the fire brigade, knitting hundreds of blankets made up of colored squares. They are used out in the field by the emergency responders when they need to comfort people who have been in traumatic car accidents or fires. I call them '*Grace blankets*' because they feel like a warm hug and are infused with her benevolent love.

I do look to her and think about her advice from time to time which helps me work towards some higher purpose. I see how she has faced her own pain and still has some light inside that she wants to shine forth. I see her demonstrate and live it but it still seems like a long stretch for me to get to the point of benevolence. Granted, she had the benefit of time and hindsight on her side but I wondered if it was possible to live a beautiful life right now in spite of the ugly events.

Like my Nan, the memory of the past two years all stayed hidden inside my body. The pressure compounded internally until it finally erupted like a volcano of heat right out of my flesh and skin. It was only a matter of time until the body could not contain the mystery anymore. A new pain was waiting to be birthed.

Twisted
Childs pose

Twisted Childs Pose

Yin Yoga is an art form and not a science because every single person has a unique expression of the self that emerges from the heart. If we focus too strongly on the intellectual it detaches us from the direct felt experience. Science is based on objective observation where art, like life, is subjective. It's ok to know the theory but it is more useful to feel it. The concept of art is that it is creative, alive and connected to your soul. It is while sitting in these shapes that you hear the voice of your inner child. Playful and light and eternally free from responsibility.

This pose means to me...

Releasing the burden of motherhood and
laying down the armour from my shoulders.

The invisible bond between holy mother and sacred child is very tangible when your own flesh and blood is in pain. Somehow their pain becomes your pain and any trauma your child experiences transfers through cyberspace into your joint shared 'ouch account'. A wireless nervous system shooting little pain-mail messages through your connected 'inner-net'. The truth is, I don't even need to get how that happens. I don't even know how I send an email to someone on the other side of the world and they receive it in an instant. But I trust that it does work and happily use technology in this way every day without thinking logically.

The child is like the catalyst that upgrades you to your new intuitive multisensory communication system. As mothers, we automatically receive our children's download of software, viruses and glitches. When they are grumpy, tired, sick or injured, our radar picks up whatever they are putting down. Maybe it's a backup security measure built into us to feel pain for our children in case they overlook it or get distracted playing, or are simply too busy to notice that they are missing a finger.

We believe our role as mothers is to try to protect our children from their pain, but really our role is to teach them that they are strong enough to deal with their pain. Because pain is as inevitable as death and taxes. If we are too fearful and not accepting of this fact, we will shield them, drug them, hold them back, warn them too often to 'be careful', and hide the truth from them. Being brave and compassionate enough not to project our fears onto our children takes a lot more courage.

Medical Intuitive Caroline Myss says this on protecting someone from pain:

'I will say that is a very foolish thing to do, well-meaning though it may be. It is a fool's move. Nobody has a right to prevent another person

from their pain, or protect them from their pain, because that is a way of growing up. It is a way of maturing. And what you're actually doing is protecting yourself from watching a person go through a transformation, and watching a person go through a maturing process. At a deeply unconscious level, you don't want to see that person grow up.'

Our kids' trauma triggers our own trauma buried in the depths of our inner ocean of memories. It's nature's way of birthing our intuition through our shared pain even if we are not ready to feel it or hear it. However painful it is though, we are never alone in our suffering even when we think we are a single lost diver in the vast dark ocean.

The initiation into motherhood unearths our fears and brings them to the surface. The purpose being to let them float up so we can acknowledge them and become lighter. Trauma runs deep through our ancestors and is passed on from mother to mother. My own children's pain is related to the generations that walked before them. The women who had babies throughout history, before birth control, before they could choose abortion and before intervention was even an option.

Intuition bends time and it becomes a strange phenomenon when we realise our stories are the same as our grandmothers. We are not just genetic blueprints of our elders but there is a shared ancestral experience of trauma that is passed down through generations. Even my own DNA was once contained inside the eggs inside my mother, who was inside my grandmother, who was somehow affected by pain during pregnancy and birth.

'All the eggs a woman will ever carry form in her ovaries when she is a four-month old fetus inside the womb of her mother. This means our cellular life as an egg begins in the womb of our grandmother. Each of us

spent five months in our Grandmother's womb, and she in turn formed within the womb of her Grandmother. We vibrate to the rhythms of our mother's blood before she herself is born.'

Layne Redmond, *When the Drummers were Women*

CHAPTER 6

THE CRUMBLING

'Yoga is not about touching your toes, it's about what you learn on the way down'

Back at work but barely surviving let alone thriving. Burnt out and exhausted, my health became worse and worse as I caught the flu twice one winter and seemed to have constant colds. Burnout was sneaky and insidious and crept up on me over time. My burnout period was a result of always racing from one thing to the next which meant that my whole life was spent rushing and being 'busy'. I admit that I was 'always on' even though I was supposedly only working part-time three days a week. Despite my conscious attempts to engage with my children I was drawn back to being online and was still checking emails and responding to text messages and organising stock on my days off. I also admit to dosing my kids with Panadol and dropping them off to daycare when I knew full well they were ill. The feeling of having to take another sick day was too much to bear despite the distress of my children and the contagion risk. I broke all the rules just so I wouldn't let people down, but in the end I was letting myself down.

My mobile would ring at around lunchtime and the childcare centre would be asking me to come and pick up my feverish baby. And somehow because I was the primary carer of the children and my husband worked evenings the responsibility seemed to always fall back on my shoulders. I would be the one to leave work at five and pick the kids up and then arrive home only to clock onto my second job, the witching hour of night shift. There was also this persistent underlying feeling of not enough. Not enough time, not enough success, not enough parenting, not enough love for myself, not enough energy, not enough sleep. Just not enough.

***

The war against myself finally comes to an end one Sunday afternoon in September of 2014. We are at our friend's place watching the footy while the kids all play together. I begin to feel strange and recognise these feelings as yet another virus making itself known to my system. I curl up on their couch and half an hour later it becomes obvious I am unwell and need to go home. I climb straight into bed and then start to shiver uncontrollably as another wave of nausea comes over me. It feels like the flu and I stay in bed until the following morning.

I manage to crawl into the GPs office later that morning. I'm weak and aching deep in my bones. My back and spine feel unreliable as if my whole skeleton is turning from solid bone to soft dough. Luckily both of my children are in childcare so I wilt inside of myself as I wait in the waiting room. It smells bad here. I think about having to call into work to request another sick day. I need a pile of medical certificates in my handbag. It would be so much more convenient if they sold them by the packet. The doctor calls me in and does her examination. The usual checks and questions which sound completely automated. She suggests I have another viral infection I probably picked up from my kids. The result being an overall summation of 'you're run down and exhausted and you need to go home and rest for a couple of days'. I am categorised into the 'tired and teary' mum box and sent on my way seven minutes later.

A couple of days goes by and my condition worsens. There is this pain that intensifies on my back. It seems to be on my spine right between my shoulder blades. It radiates around the left side of my torso. My whole body throbs and is full of unfamiliar sensations. As I lie in bed this realisation hits me that something serious is happening. I have never felt this type of pain before. It hurts to move, it hurts to breathe and it hurts to think. Whatever darkness has a hold of me wants me to pay attention. So I do what anyone would do with an electronic device within reach. I type up 'Dr Google' and begin my own research and diagnosis into the reason why I may be dying. 'Flu', 'Nerve Pain' 'One side' 'Virus' 'Back pain...' shingles?

I go back to my GP two days later and she examines me again, this time noticing two spots on my spine. 'This could be shingles', she says. Because the common skin rash is so small it was misdiagnosed. The poison or neurotoxin from the virus didn't so much move outward to the peripheral nerves and skin, but instead travelled inwards into the larger nerves and spinal column creating an even greater strain on my immune system. Yes, it was indeed shingles. Shingles is caused by the *zoster* virus, which is a species in the herpes family. It's an attack on the nervous system and known as one of the most intensely painful conditions in our western medical community. She gives me anti-viral medication to prevent the complication of postherpetic neuralgia (ongoing nerve pain that lasts longer than a month), however by this stage due to the delayed diagnosis we have missed the window of less than 72 hours since the onset. I missed my chance. So my only option is to manage the pain. I am sent home with all the drugs and instructed to take them round the clock. One of these drugs is a steroid which I later discover actually weakens your immune system, therefore giving shingles the opportunity to further reproduce and become a stronger invader. A double blow to my health.

For the first four weeks of the virus my days consist of sleeping and 'barely parenting'. I am taking opiates for the pain so I can get some relief and function as a mother to pick the girls up from daycare. I remember from both births how I tolerated it well so it becomes my primary line of care. If it wears off or I forget to take it on time I curl up in the fetal position and sob until the drug takes affect and numbness kicks into my system an hour later. I want answers from my doctor on when I will heal. Like most working parents feel, I don't have time for all this recovering. Just give me a number. Three months? Six? I learn that everyone has expectations for the estimation of my recovery. Employers, family and doctors all reassure me I just need to take one day at a time. Their thoughts are based on nothing but guesses and short time frames to give me hope. I feel let down by my body. My mind wants absolutes and deadlines desperately trying to control the situation.

As chronic fatigue sets in life demands that I surrender to being sick. My willingness to medicate the pain with the opiates I am prescribed is now the only control I have. It is as though the universe is speaking to me saying *rest now*, feel it, *let go*. But my ego won't have it. I am not a great sufferer.

Over this time my whole identity and personality dissolves as I lay flat on my back for weeks. Who I thought I was, no longer exists. This illness is taking something from me and about to alter the trajectory of my life. It is a mystical experience of letting go and surrendering to everything that has shaped me up until this point. I know in my bones that there is greater meaning to this pain as a result of me ignoring all the physical warning signs. It is simply my time because there is only so much blocking of your intuition you can do until something breaks. In my case it is my nervous system.

One Sunday morning I find myself going to a Yin Yoga class. I read somewhere that Yin Yoga includes all floor based stretches and is very slow and healing for the nervous system. This is exactly what I need. There is no way I'm able to do any weight bearing poses like downward facing dog. Anything that involves putting pressure or engaging the muscles around my back will risk fatigue and pain. I'm nervous it is going to cause a flare up but I can't exist inside of this stiff and rigid body. My shoulders are frozen up around my ears. My face wears the mask of pain etching tension in the wrinkles across my forehead. There are new lines around my eyes and mouth from constantly clenching my jaw and grinding my teeth. My world has shrunk so much I'm a smaller version of myself in an unrecognisable body.

The smell of incense permeates the space as I walk nervously into the Yoga studio. Fragrances of the earth mixed with musk fill my nostrils as I take my shoes off. Candles flicker on the windowsill ledges and the sound of singing bowls reverberates in the background. There is something about walking with bare feet that starts the process of unravelling tension. I find a space and roll out my mat next to a neat row of other mats being careful to line it up so I don't overstep any boundaries. I observe people around me talking closely, hugging, stretching, meditating or simply lying down. I notice one girl standing on her head so effortlessly she could be hanging out at a bar sipping a pina colada. I'm equally impressed and intimidated by her physical prowess.

As soon as the teacher Clare, begins to start the class I am immediately relieved.

"Close your eyes and release all your worries," she says. The darkness is comforting and behind my eyes my reality ceases to matter.

"Feel the floor under your back and notice where you are

connected to the earth" she suggests. I have not connected to my body in a long time. I have spent a good deal of effort deliberately trying to disconnect from my body. Numbing it so it can do what it wants and what it has to do to appear capable and in control. It takes so much energy to put up this front every day. I invest most of my time trying to ignore my body and its pain. As I lie in stillness in the dark I realise there is nowhere to run to. Something drew me into Yoga to connect. My eyes are still closed and I breathe deeply, feeling the air swell my torso like a welcome wind.

Clare continues with her job of guiding me, providing a safe familiar voice to hook into.

"You have permission to put down your burdens," she says. Whatever is weighing me down, my attachments, my thoughts, my guilt, I have permission to put it down? This class immediately proves to be more than just exercise. I feel space and a quiet inside that is almost echoing between my ears.

Tears are pushing at the back of my throat. I need to cry but I can't seem to muster enough tragedy to spill them over the edge. I'm too numb with medication to actually feel anything real and I can't break down the chemical barriers that block and hold the hurt in. Memories, events, frustration, resentment and anguish want to surge out of me but remain trapped underneath my skin. Even feeling sorry for my dry eye situation is not enough oomph to push the tears out. I look down at my unpolished toenails and sigh out loud a pathetic sound you make when you are clumsy and drop something repeatedly.

After an hour and a half of stillness, stretching and breathing, for the first time ever I lie in Savasana face up in a room full of people imitating corpses. I enjoy this feeling of playing dead and being allowed to vacate my body as if it is a hotel room. I leave the dirty towels on the floor and my bed unmade for room service as if I can check out and return to a fresh new experience of living. Clare moves behind my head and rubs a sweet smelling oil into my scalp and temples. I am temporarily transported to another planet. The touch of her human skin on mine mixed with sweat creates a sense of pleasure I am surprised to receive. It's like the energy of compassion is being infused through the hairs on my head and I'm receiving a gift from the heavens. The opposite feeling of pain hovers over me and for a moment I know I am going to be OK. It's not magic, it's much more grounded than that. The pills offer me magic contained in white powder. This is something much more real. It is not made up of longing and wishing and waving a wand, it is a spark of grace. Right here in Savasana as I lie on deaths door, the tears stream down my face, and at last, drip lovingly over my chin.

Lying Spinal Twist Pose

Lying Spinal Twist Pose

Yin Yoga is earth honouring and feminine based. The source of our spirit is The Great Mother because we are born out of the feminine. Remembering Mother nature inside of us returns our awareness to the creator and helps us feel into our divine feminine power. We have never lost it.

This pose means to me...

Reclaiming my woman centre and rinsing away everything I have given away my power to.

The rushing and the stressing and the juggling of too many tasks was blocking my Intuition. My intuition was trying to tell me to slow down. Even old ladies in the street would stop me and say 'Enjoy this time in your life it all goes by so fast'. It annoyed me so much because I wasn't enjoying it, and so I therefore felt like there was something fundamentally wrong with me.

My Intuition was trying to tell me first through my gut and the constant queasiness. I dismissed it as the common feeling of 'mother guilt' many women embody as a result of spreading themselves to thin. But it wasn't guilt, it was love trying to get through to me. Intuitive hits are sourced from divine energy which simply want you to make balanced choices based on truth and love. However, I blocked all that guidance and instead pushed through when I was being asked to *just stop*. Stop and reassess your life here. What is really going on?

Sometimes (often, actually), we need something bigger to stop us in our tracks and really pay attention. Perhaps even a little shock. Eventually, the universal law of balance will prevail and deliver what we need in the form of illness to redirect our compass so we are forced to take a real close look at our behavior.

To heal this and to get out of survival mode, we need to turn towards our intuition and away from the myth of the superwoman. We were fed a lie. We cannot *have it all* but we can *intuit it all*. We can embrace a much more feminine energy when it comes to our work, our families, our attitudes and our beliefs. We can instead tap into the memory that we contain our own power instead of conforming to patriarchal structures. It's a humorous aspect of being human that we forget how powerful we are as women, both individually and as a group. Waging a war against our maternal instincts is exhausting and tiring and quite frankly, becoming very unfunny.

Chronic pain can be a result of being in survival fight or flight for too long. It changes a person and shakes you internally, mixing up all your beliefs until you don't recognise them anymore. It forces you to look at life with much more openness because you can't remember what it was like to be physically strong. Until your health is taken away from you, you have to find your confidence somewhere other than your physical body. So naturally your attention shifts to the mind and the spirit. The other parts of you that make up a whole person, which we often neglect in our culture.

As women, we need to become empowered to look holistically within and honour the fact that feminine health is unique. Can we see that the 'I'm tired' doesn't mean there is something 'wrong' with us, but rather a natural need for rest. Not an excuse to judge ourselves and push through or soldier on. This is exactly what blocks us from intuitively flowing with our cycles and hormonal changes as well as our ability to heal.

Dr Christiane Northrup writes an eloquent article on the Medicine for Empowerment in which she stresses the importance of being mindful of the feminine difference...

'As a physician, I've seen time and time again how our inner guidance also comes in the form of bodily symptoms and illnesses – especially when we are living lives devoid of pleasure, joy, and hope. Our illnesses are designed to stop us in our tracks, make us rest, and bring our attention back to the things that are really important and that give our lives meaning and joy – aspects of life that we often put on the back burner until "someday". The insights catalyzed by decades of medical practice as well as my own health problems challenged everything I learned at medical school and residency training about womens' health. Over the years, it became abundantly clear to me that premenstrual syndrome (PMS), pelvic pain, fibroid tumours, chronic vaginitis, breast problems and menstrual cramps were related to the contexts of an individual woman's life and her beliefs about herself and what she thought was possible in her life. All of these factors are associated with very real biochemical changes in our cells. Learning about their diets,

work situations and relationships often provided me with clues to the source of a patient's distress – and, more important, what steps needed to be taken to relieve that distress. Over the years, I have learned to appreciate the thoughts, beliefs and behavioural patterns behind medical conditions in ways that simply aren't addressed in medical training. These insights are the missing link to optimal health on all levels.'

It became very clear to me that my intuition was speaking to me through my illness in my body. The chronic pain was there because of unresolved trauma, my beliefs about myself not being enough, the stress of all the 'doing' and trying to please others. The immediate relief through the nerves on my back followed the moment my tears hit my chin. Without my emotional pain there would be no physical pain because the two were inextricably linked. However, the doctors were simply fixated on the part of me that they could see with their eyes, not the invisible emotions which were moving energy around my body.

The truth was I was trying to do everything on my own because I was an independent woman of course. This is how my generation of young women were raised. I grew up in the 80s when young girls were told they could do anything and be anything. My parents encouraged me to do it all. To be highly educated, get good grades, be financially independent, have a successful career, a loving marriage, produce another generation, and not shy away from hard work. We had the right to choose but it came at a cost.

I'm pretty sure my mother's experience of raising my sister and I was different. I came close to disappearing a few times as a kid but it didn't stop my parents from allowing us to explore the neighborhood until dark. I spent many hours of my childhood walking the streets of our suburb unattended, building cubbies in the bush and chasing animals around the block. The only rule was to come home before dark when the street lights turned on. Sure there were bruises, cuts and the odd stitches required but, in hindsight, those lessons were worth all of those carefree hours. They taught me that adventure and exploration is essential for the spirit, and that I'm a strong survivor. There was a freedom for both parents and children that is extinct now.

As a mother now I would like to rebel against the extreme helicopter movement that poses a threat to what many would describe as the basic rights of childhood. The challenge for us is to use our intuition to find the point of balance between protecting our children and allowing them enough freedom to discover their world. Our kids will suffer the occasional injury and we need to view this as normal otherwise we are communicating to them that any pain is to be avoided and is wrong.

So much of our life is *beyond our control*, and as long as we protect our children from this fact we will create suffering for them. Being overprotective means we will raise frustrated rebels, nervous wrecks and a pain resistant generation.

The pressure to perform and achieve drives the reason for many women crumbling. The tower comes crashing down because we try to be all things to all people. For this unrealistic expectation all we get is exhaustion, infertility, insomnia, hormone imbalance, anxiety, depression and burnout. We are left wondering why the tower crumbles which translates into 'I am not enough'. In a desperate effort to never experience this feeling of shame around self-worth and *not being enough* we create adaptive coping strategies. Numbing and distracting ourselves through overworking and overachieving is a popular survival response. But the memory of the pain of our childhood conditioning remains and the issues are still in our tissues.

The Sanskrit word 'Yoga' actually means to 'Yoke'. It is the joining or connection between the body, the mind and the spirit. Why was I not yoked? I dived right into this question, so much so, that I developed a passion and curiosity for it which consumed me and was a welcome distraction from the pain. My definition of success was changing after years of being in the corporate world. Even though my employer was supportive of me throughout the process, I knew the career had run its course. Even though there was still a fear around 'Who am I if my identity is not caught up in this job title?' I knew I would be unsuccessful if I stayed working in it. I remember a quote that says 'the crack is where the light gets in', and once you get a taste of the light in all your brokenness, even if it's just for a moment, it sparks a purpose inside of you which renders your old job unbearable and pointless. The light being the healing power of Yoga and my longing to share it with others. So the work had to change. I made the decision on a Sunday to resign and walked into the office the following Monday morning and did it. Intuition demands fast decisions and action.

***

Allowing myself to live a slower life was liberating. Everything changed once I was free and embraced the reduced pace. I enrolled in a Yoga teacher training course which sent me on a mission to find out as much as possible about this healing science. I read the thousand year old texts and sacred scriptures as part of my teacher training and learnt the original yogis knew a thing or two about this 'yoking' process. It excited me so much I had to consciously hold myself back from learning and even practicing too much Yoga too fast. Out of habit I wanted to work hard at my new passion, however, I knew how much I could do safely without getting overwhelmed and triggering pain flare ups. This delicate balance required a deep listening to my intuition and a level of trust to follow it when it nudged me to stop. New choices to live a simpler life at home changed to support my nervous system as well. My parenting changed as I really learnt to pick my battles with the kids and taught them more independence. I also called for more help from babysitters, cleaners and family. Healing really became an art of living over a science.

Tina Bruce

7th birthday
Dad kisses

In my mother's arms

Dad's little helpers

Wedding Byron Bay

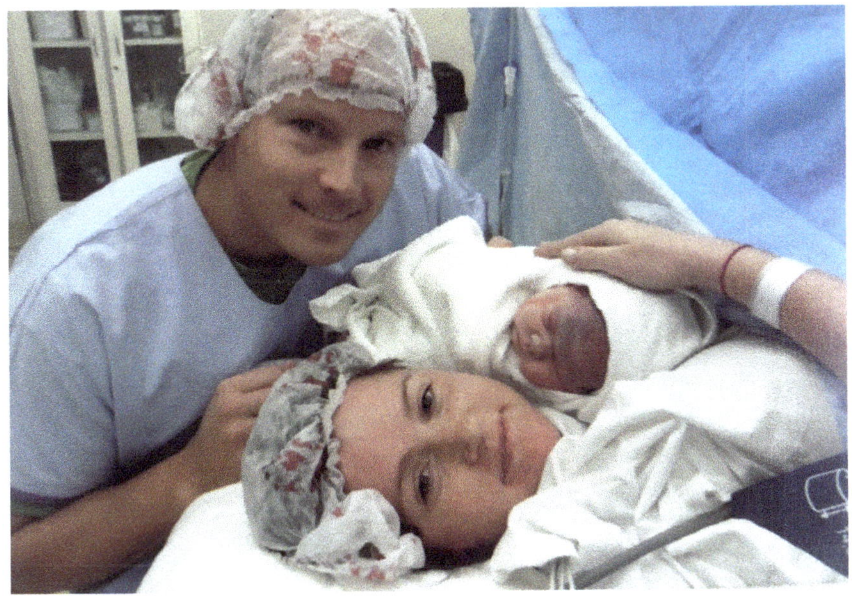

Leila May crashes into the world

Family life begins...

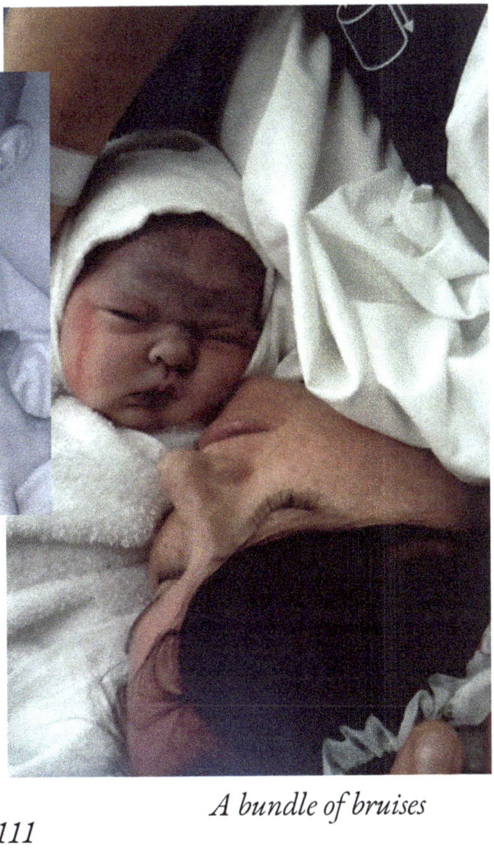

A bundle of bruises

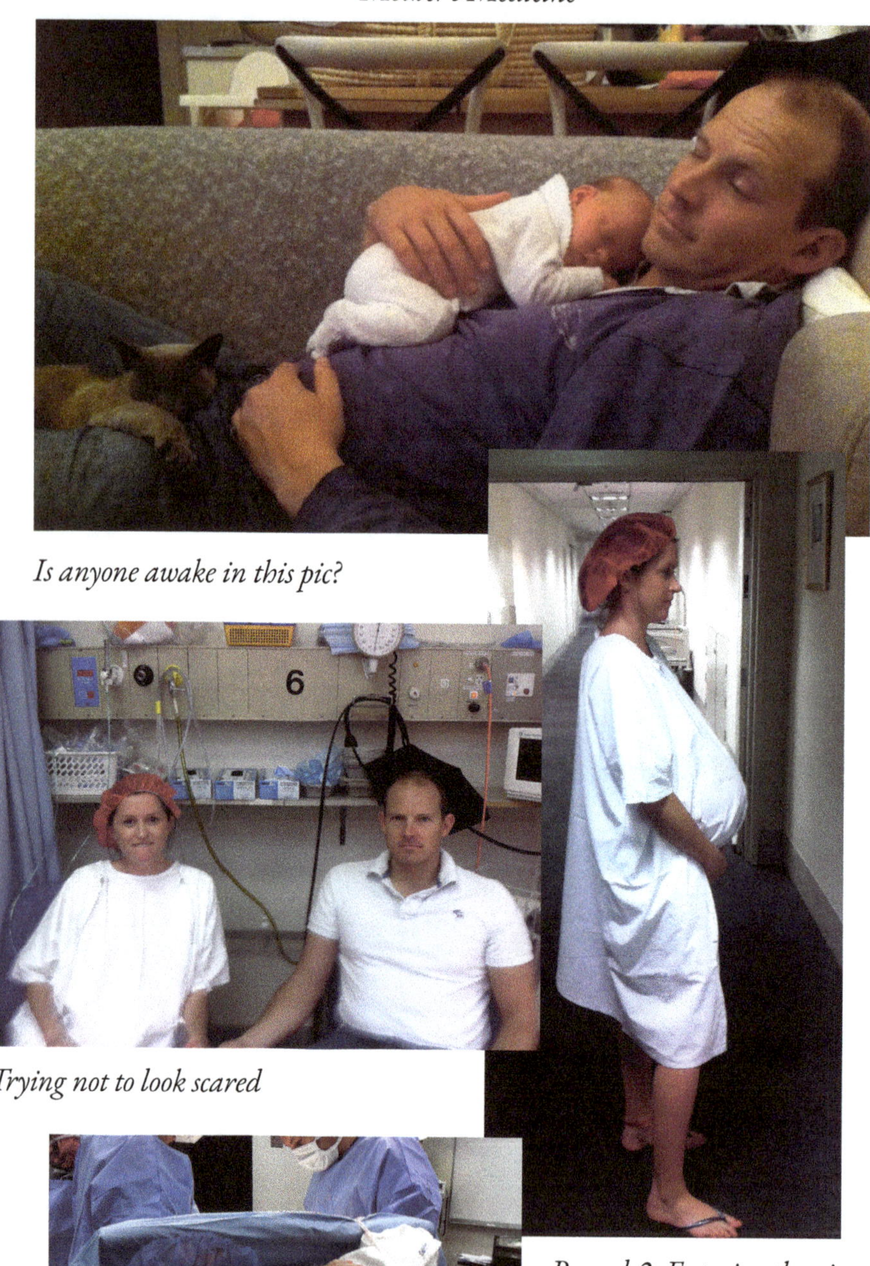

Is anyone awake in this pic?

Trying not to look scared

Round 2. Entering the ring

Zoë Berry is born!

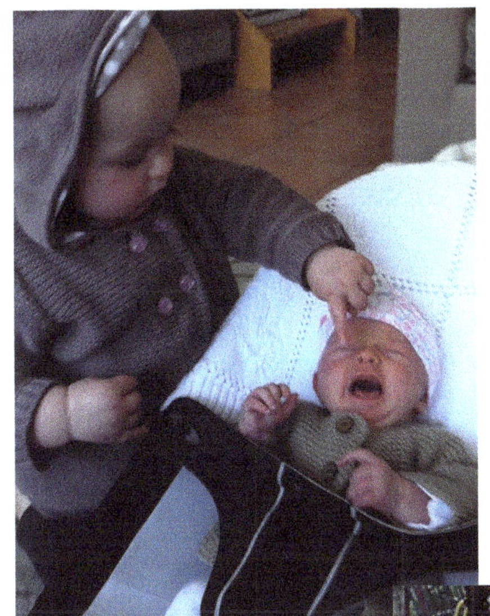

The daily push

It was love at first poke

Xtreme parenting as a sport

2 little monkeys

Pain becomes her

Healing four generations

Finding my Yogi

Bonza! Found my spirit

India calls

Grace in Greece

This day

CHAPTER 7

LOOKING UP

*'Which do you want,
the pain of staying where you are,
or the pain of growth?'*

The pain was still there constantly. In fact, it was increasing as I was diagnosed with *Postherpetic Neuralgia* which is the ongoing chronic pain condition that lives on in the nerve fibres once the shingles rash has gone. More common in people over the age of sixty so rare and unexpected in a young woman, unless they were carrying a significant amount of stress and trauma inside.

The pain was no longer a symptom of the shingles virus though. The pain had actually become its own disease. The pain had 'chronified' but was impossible to see and measure. Taking an image such as an x-ray or MRI would not reveal anything abnormal. It was totally invisible which meant I looked okay on the outside but my inner world was torn apart. It was as though my nervous system was similar to the electric wiring in a house and somebody had broken in and removed the insulation layers that protected the cables and switched them all around. Every time the wires bumped or strained they electrocuted my flesh and bones. Nobody could see the wiring behind the walls of each room, but if you switched on the light in the kitchen, the bathroom light would turn on instead. My wires were crossed and nothing was communicating effectively so as a result I became super sensitive to noise, stimulation, lights, people, temperature and wind, strangely enough.

So the drug became my insulation layer and kept me safe. It did its best to protect me but it was setting me up for yet another disease. The dis-ease of addiction.

One morning I woke up in greater than usual agonising pain. It felt like someone was stabbing me between the shoulder blades while I was carrying around a 30 kilogram backpack. The weight was so overbearing that I returned home from a day at work and literally had to crawl up the stairs on my hands and knees. The kids actually thought this was a game so I tried to make light of it, however, I was hanging out for the extra dose of opiates to kick in so I could get through the evening witching hour.

The plan was to taper off the opiates slowly. I was given a schedule from the doctor and the pharmacist on how to wean away the chemicals my body had become dependent on. The opiate receptors in my brain needed to adjust to the reduced drug amount. I would attempt to start the day drug free, but I would last only until about 1 pm when the inconvenient nerve pain rendered me dysfunctional. Then the next dose would need to be twice as much just to touch the sides of the pain. So the merry-go-round continued of pain, pill, sleep, pain, pill. My dependence on opioids was entirely predictable given the duration I was prescribed it for.

This time though, the opiate was wearing off much faster. I needed more of the drug for it to be effective. From when I first started taking it, I had increased my dose from two capsules to six. Sometimes seven or eight. I was in despair. Saddened by my own hopelessness, I went to my Yoga mat as the sun was rising and collapsed in desperation. I didn't want to be the grey version of myself anymore. Chained to these pills which controlled every minute of every day of my thoughts. What time will I take the next one? Can I have just one more? Will I wake up in the morning if I have another one? Will the doctor give me another script? Not being able to leave the house without these pills. They began to control my life.

I started to go 'doctor shopping'; getting multiple scripts from different GPs, always omitting the truth of how much I was actually taking. I was filled with shame and guilt. I had given over my power to these pills and I wanted so badly to get off the them but the withdrawal symptoms were so severe it made it seemingly impossible.

Two years since the shingles diagnosis and I was still going back to the GP regularly to get my script for Tramadol repeated again and again. Every time I returned I knew what the doctor was going to say. It got to the point when she really didn't know how to help me anymore. I even caught her rolling her eyes to the reception staff upon seeing me in the waiting room one afternoon. Her humiliating reaction was merely a reflection of her inability to solve a problem in the confined five-minute consulting window she was allowed. She didn't understand. She believed in logic and reason and cause and effect. To her, pain was about rational problems and solutions. What she didn't take into account was that my problem had become irrational.

When she called my name I kept my eye gaze low and followed her like a shrunken version of myself I no longer recognised. She sat down and stared straight ahead at her computer screen while hammering away at the keys robotically. Her stiff head fixed her eyes on the words and assessment she was already typing before she even opened her mouth. She looked at me that day and asked me to explain why I was there.

"I'm here to refill my script for Tramadol," I confessed.

"I know you have been to see other doctors around this area to get scripts. Dr X rang me and told me you were there on Saturday 'doctor shopping' for Tramadol," she said. I had been caught out like a guilty thief. I was desperate because any slight reduction in my medication as a result of running out would throw me into withdrawal which would mean I would become too sick to care for the kids.

Doctor shopping is now recorded amongst postcodes and suburbs like an online network. I imagined my face plastered all over a closed Facebook group of GPs warning: 'Do not serve this woman. She is desperate and dangerous to herself.'

I was now the subject of a drug neighborhood watch and terrified of telling the truth because deep down, I believed child services might come along and take my kids away from me and deem me grossly unfit as a parent. I was an irresponsible addict who dragged her children around and exposed them to doctors surgeries and pharmacies looking for her next hit. What if they put me away, or even worse, separated me from my family? I did doubt whether I could look after my children responsibly because I saw myself as weak and pathetic and untrustworthy. I was frightened I would be locked away. The idea of being an inadequate mother was plaguing me.

She then turned her whole body towards me as if her neck was wrapped around a steel rod and said she didn't know how to help me anymore so she was going to refer me to a specialist. I knew in the absence of any physical evidence I was at risk of being diagnosed with 'hysteria'. Originally named after the 'wandering womb' thousands of years ago. The Greeks called it 'Hysteria' – from Hystera, or Uterus – and believed women were generally 'crazy', over reactive and emotional when it came to their own health. This label being exclusive to females was becoming a real possibility for me. That naughty womb of mine was not behaving again. The term was only officially dropped from the medical bible in the early 1950s so there could still be groups of hysterical women out there, alive, loose and free roaming the streets. I wondered if she was going to turn the hose on me but instead I got turned out onto the street.

Less than ten minutes later I walked out of the medical clinic and hopped into my car sobbing. I felt woefully alone. She didn't have time to truly listen to me. I felt like I had failed somehow. I was passed on to a neurologist. This specialist doctor prescribed me more drugs and just wanted to double my dose of neuropathic painkillers. Her theory was if we covered the pain completely with medication then my overactive pain signals would unlearn their hypersensitivity. The side effects of these medications (which are also prescribed for people with epilepsy) included crazy mental fogginess, drowsiness, weight gain and memory loss. I couldn't make decisions or function, let alone stay awake so I refused to take them. There wasn't one doctor that could show me exactly what I needed to do. There had to be another way.

***

How was I to break the pill popping cycle? It took a scare and divine intervention for another solution. One night as I drifted easily off into my regular night time state of opiate drowsiness, conveniently useful for falling asleep, I fell asleep too hard. Falling asleep too hard results in waking up suddenly gasping for breath. They call this respiratory depression, which is common when there is a build up of narcotics in the system and both the breathing rate and heart rate suspend momentarily. It was as if my soul knew that if I remained asleep that night I would not wake up in the morning. It took every ounce of its soul power to open my eyes and shake me out of this dream state so I could breathe again. One giant gasp and I was wide awake, alert, panicked and shaken for the remainder of the night. I took the same amount of medication I did most days so the fact that my body reacted differently this time meant this pill regime had become unpredictable and life threatening.

Once I had absorbed the holy-fuck of it all, my only reaction then was to flush the pills down the loo, plummeting me swiftly into acute withdrawal symptoms. My neuralgia started to increase and burn like wildfire. Raw nerves just flapping in the breeze sensitive to every touch, sight and sound. The air hurt me. And then on top of that, within 24 hours I began to shake with cold chills. It felt like a really bad flu. Everything ached like a bone-deep soreness to the core. The nausea kicked in. My stomach churned and I could feel the acidic taste in my mouth rising on queue to vomit ferociously. There was no energy to walk without having to take breaks just to catch my breath. My unbearable restless legs and anxiety would not allow me to sleep.

Turns out, opiate withdrawal is a living nightmare! This is pretty common knowledge however surely this sort of punishment is only reserved for heroin addicts. I'm a mother for Christ's sake! An honest human being trying to do the right thing and just following doctor's orders. My victim inside of me was crying out "Why is this happening to me?!" As the days went on my symptoms got a lot worse. My internal thermostat was non existent. I couldn't seem to get warm one second and then the next would break into a cold sweat. But the most disturbing thing was that things began to get very dark.

The depression, anxiety and hallucinations made me feel paranoid and displaced. I couldn't really control the tremors and jitters that took over my body and found it increasingly difficult to hide my pain. With that came utter hopelessness and the shame was so smothering I didn't know how to reach out for help. I ended up resorting to climbing into bed and confessing to my kids, 'Mummy feels sick again'. I did such a great job at constantly hiding my pain that they accepted my 'bad back' as part of the package I came in.

I must have attempted one hundred times to wean off the medication prescribed to me. I woke up each morning thinking 'today is going to be the day', only to crumble within hours, unable to cope. The tapering was obviously too aggressive but part of the problem was my impatience. It was like going slowly down in dose was too big a temptation to stay on the pills. I knew they were either burning a hole in my handbag or just a prescription away from being filled. They would call me and beg to put an end to the suffering. *You don't deserve to suffer like this. Why don't you carry me around in your handbag just in case? Just take one to take the edge off the withdrawal.* They took on a magnetism far greater than their teeny little size breaking any willpower I had. Of course I wanted to go back on the pills. I was in agony. Hell who was I kidding? I had no power. The pills had all the power. These orange and white capsules filled with white powder. I began to believe I would never recover. Withdrawing while raising children is known to be extremely tough...but so is raising them from a morgue. I did not want to die. It was time to pray.

So at 5 o'clock one morning, I dropped to my knees and started to pray. I looked up instinctively. Not left or right or down, but up towards the sky. Why do we look up in that direction when we pray? I didn't logically know what to do but it's as if intuition knew exactly what it needed to do. It was just waiting for me to finally surrender and get out of my own way so it could find its source of power and get to work. Grace was ready to swoop on in. I was no expert in prayer vocabulary so it went a bit like this...

"Holy hell this hurts. God? if you have any influence at all up there I'd appreciate some help. Fuck this hurts. I can't go on anymore. I am handing over this pain now."

"I have officially reached the end of myself. I give up trying to fix this. Unless you come up with something I will stay on these drugs forever if that is what I have to do. I've tried to do this on my own and it doesn't work. I have got nothing left. I'm in your hands," I sobbed. I then proceeded to swallow three pills and went downstairs for breakfast.

Sleeping Swan
Pose

Sleeping Swan Pose

Yin Yoga uses animal shapes as a way of relating to human nature. Most important is the spirit that moves through each animal posture containing the energy of that creature. Animals don't overthink things, they exist and act intuitively. By doing this you can create a shape based on a living being merging your consciousness with theirs.

This pose means to me...

A swan is graceful, majestic and fluidly moves with the water not fighting the currents. Opening up your hips in this posture enables you to move and walk with more ease and flow. It's about dropping the stories that restrict you.

How does one live with chronic pain? Not very well or at least not without a lot of chemical assistance in my case. *Persistent pain* can be like having a giant hole in your soul. It is so relentless that it's not a matter of *if* it breaks your spirit but *when*. And then you enter the rich territory of rock bottom which is a privileged place to be.

The biggest disservice to myself during my rock bottom was my inability to ask for help. It always seemed easier to just do things myself rather than admit defeat. I can see now this was a symptom of the trauma; keeping shame well and truly hidden from public viewing. When you are in a fight or flight response chronically you don't ask for help because that would require you to be vulnerable and your body doesn't allow that to happen.

I was being pulled to explore the other parts of myself that I needed to lean on to get me through this struggle. Desperation made the decision for me to listen for guidance, counsel or instruction. I knew if I created the space for it, I might hear something. A voice, a sound, a feeling, a knowing, anything that would tell me what my next move could be to dig myself out of the ditch.

Intuition has to step forward and the longer we block it the more drastic its attempts become to gain our attention.

So how do we actually know what voice is? Is it my ego or my soul? Each one has very different agendas so discernment is key.

Here are some *truth clues...*

1. When you ignore your intuition the same person or situation will keep on triggering you. You will continue to be annoyed by them or it, because it's simply reflecting back to you what you refuse to look at within.
2. Your ego is generally a negative noisy voice you hear repetitively in your head. I have two gremlins that reside in my brain which team up and collude. One is called '*you don't have enough time*' and the other one is called '*what will people think?*' Any time I hear those

voices I know it is not my wise woman.

3. Your ego will make you feel like you are being squeezed or squashed. Paralysed with indecision. Your intuition will make you feel certain. Big. Expansive. Light.
4. Your ego will resist trying something new. It likes to keep you safe and small. It likes you to choose the path of least resistance. Your intuition wants you to take some sort of risk or leap. It won't be certain of the outcome but it will want to play the game regardless and be a participant IN the world, not OF the world.
5. When following your intuition synchronicity will begin to present itself everywhere as your outside world begins to mirror your more authentic inside world. You will meet people who want to play the game with you. Opportunities will start to come your way.
6. When you make the true decision you will be exhausted by the process but it will be a happy exhaustion. And then there is NO turning back. Once you have crossed that line there is no room for doubt. It's only onwards and upwards.
7. Finally, a daily practice of shutting down the eyes and sitting in silence will prepare you to fine tune your instrument. When you become open and ready to receive, you're in business.

"*The past is in your head. The future is in your hands.*"
Buddha

CHAPTER 8

PALOMA

'Each morning we are born again. What we do today is what matters most'

A few hours after my early morning prayer, something peculiar occurred. The name 'Paloma' downloaded into my brain.

"Paloma? What on earth is Paloma?" I thought. It sounded like 'pavlova'. I muddled around for a couple more hours and eventually my inner voice could not be silenced. I googled 'Paloma' 'Melbourne' and low and behold, this person was a doctor and existed in my neighbourhood! I found her mobile listed on the website and rang her on a Saturday. Not realising it was her day off work and this was probably not an appropriate time to introduce myself, I called.

A woman - Paloma - answered the call.

"Who is this? How did you get my number?" she demanded.

"I found it on the internet," I replied meekly. I went on to explain my situation and she could hear the desperation in my voice. I had been taking Tramadol every day for two years because my current GP prescribed it to me and thought this was ok. She had told me she had a patient on this drug indefinitely because he had a really bad back and who was she to judge? The prescriber I would have thought. This particular GP also referred me to a 'pain specialist' psychologist however she was unable to help me six months and $6000 later. By the time I rang Paloma that Saturday morning I was ready to go into an inpatient rehab facility.

"Come into my office at 2pm on Monday. On one condition. You have to bring your husband with you," Paloma said quickly.

"Thank you, we'll be there," I replied.

Monday morning arrived and Oli and I were ready. For the first time I felt relieved that he knew the full extent of what was going on and was there by my side to support me. It helped to diffuse the shame which consumed me on a constant basis.

Her office was tucked away in a back street and we entered with hope and trepidation. Her waiting room had posters of addiction hotlines, AA meetings and support groups. There were 'drop-ins' waiting to see her who were clearly from dire situations and commission flat occupants. We looked 'normal' and a bit out of place in comparison. But I bet looking around the waiting room that those patients were thinking they were the 'normal' ones and we weren't.

At this point I had to acknowledge that in many ways, despite all my best efforts, I had failed myself. I had to realise that it was ok to ask for help. I felt deep shame even though it wasn't my fault. I still felt like I was in some way to blame for the birth, the illness and the addiction. My dependence on this drug enabled me to function 'normally' as a mother and a wife, however, I was far from normal. I was scared. My intuition was telling me Paloma could be trusted though so towards her door we walked.

She called us into her office and straight away I sensed her confidence. She oozed confidence in a no-bullshit kind of way. Like she had seen it ALL before. There was no pulling the wool over this woman's eyes. She had sharp intuition. She needed it too I was guessing by the looks of her patients in the waiting room. Judging by her audience she had some useful expertise in mental health and drugs. Lots of drugs.

I told her exactly every detail from the shingles to today. I told her I had been taking the opiates every day for two years and my other GP said it would be okay to take these for the rest of my life if I needed. My GP said that Tramadol was not addictive like other opiates. The company drug reps told her this fact, which is ironic considering I used to be a drug rep and knew we worked like robots just regurgitating what we were told to say by the big name pharmaceutical businesses.

I could tell Paloma was biting her lip and trying to withhold her opinion of that statement.

I went on to explain I'd also seen a neurologist, a psychologist and pain specialist, none of which had been able to get me off these drugs. I told her I was prepared to go into a rehab facility today if she thought it would be the best solution.

She looked at us directly and said:

"How much are you taking?"

"About 300 mg of Tramadol a day," I responded,

"Maybe more." It was more like 400mg but I always gave the most conservative answer. Just like you would as a woman if someone asked you how many men have you slept with your entire life. Underestimate your answer in fear of judgement just to be safe. Except there was no point with Paloma.

"So you are taking maximum 400 mg per day," she stated.

"How did she know that?" I thought. Intuition as sharp as whip can sniff out a lie from a layman.

"You are parents right? How old are your children? I can get you off these pills today if you work together as a family," she stated matter-of-factly.

Never had a doctor suggested this radical thought. "Together? You mean I don't need to go through this alone, the star of my own shame shit show?" I thought.

Up until now I had the leading role in the movie of 'Me'. It was a silent internal movie. The exact type of movie that fuels characters such as 'shame' and makes them famous celebrities. My shame character was a real diva. She demanded attention and pleasure and nothing but the finest white powder. Even if she needed to lie and go on a doctor shopping spending spree to get her hands on it. She recoiled at the slightest twinge of pain. Shutting down that part of herself like it was an annoying uncle. She had me working on-call and round the clock to meet her incessant needs. She particularly loved it when I hid the pills and took them only in private, behind closed doors. Never could anyone witness this type of behavior. Divas live in the dark.

Paloma leant forward and looked at me.

"Tina, two years is too long to be taking these pills every day," she said seriously. This was the first time I had heard a GP say this. All my effort to get off opioids up until now had been at my own request. I requested a referral to see a specialist. I requested a mental health plan to see a psychologist. I requested to be sent to a pain clinic. None of which helped. It wasn't really clear whose job it was to manage me until I came face to face with this woman.

Paloma had a plan.

"Have you tried Lyrica?" she asked.

"Yes, but I didn't like the side effects of fuzzy head," I said.

Paloma's immediate intention was to interrupt the circuit in my brain that was consuming me around when to take the next pill. My behavior around anticipating and constantly strategising my own medical management was sending me dangerously bonkers.

"You are in my hands now. I'm going to put you on a low dose Buprenorphine patch. It is a slow release and lasts for seven days and will keep you out of withdrawal," she said.

A solution - hurrah! My previous GP did not know that these existed. Even though Buprenorphine or Suboxone is technically an opiate, the effect of having a patch I could set and forget would at least give me a chance to break the habit of popping pills and chasing the next dose the entire day. Maybe that would open up the possibility to mend the hole in my soul. Maybe it would give me space to actually talk. Maybe I would get a chance to realise my own Mother's Medicine was directing me to heal but I simply couldn't feel it because I was numb. Unfortunately in society pain patches are used as a replacement not an opportunity but with the right intention and guidance they can be helpful. Replacing an addiction with another addiction was not the ideal solution, however, in my case, the addiction was not the fundamental problem. The fundamental problem was the pain that I was trying to escape.

She then put me on a lower dose of Lyrica to minimise the side effects. And finally she gave Oli a script for the opiate pills. Only in case of an emergency. Control is in his nature so I think he enjoyed being the gatekeeper and having this very important job of legal drug dealer.

As it turned out I didn't need the emergency pills. I made a couple of desperate phone calls to my husband but he was able to deflect my cravings. Deliberately not answering his phone and calling me back an hour later. This infuriated me but I see he was just giving me time to see if I could let the craving pass. Paloma's strategy was successful in managing the withdrawal symptoms. It was by no means easy and still required courage and stamina like no other but I was very grateful. She created some space for me to heal my relationship with my pain. Even though initially I thought I would only be on the patch for six weeks this actually turned into one whole year. This goes to show how healing takes time. Even though our ego always wants to rush our healing, the message again and again from the universe is to surrender.

My senses began slowly returning to me. It was only now that I could really begin the required work on myself to get to the root cause of all this pain. Underneath 'the patch' was still a deep wound. It was merely a Band-Aid for all my subconscious fears feeding THE pain. So my next step was to get beyond the physical treatments and get into my mind, my heart and my spirit. Throughout this entire process my Yoga mat was there for me. It held me every day as I unravelled, moved, meditated and prayed. The Mother's Medicine grew from here. My intuition was leading me to more healers and revealing more layers.

I've always thought it was synchronicity that made me pick up the phone that Saturday to call Paloma. Famous Jungian analyst, Carl Jung would describe it as part of his concept to explain meaningful events that have no known Newtonian cause.

'The accidental meeting that changes a life, the prophetic dream, the accurate intuition.'

We were a team now on the search for my power. I have since understood that the name 'Paloma' is Spanish for the word *'dove'*. A symbol of peace of the deepest kind. The dove's role is as a spiritual messenger who is sent to soothe and quieten our troubled thoughts to renew silence of the mind. A dove had arrived and taken me under her wing. For the first time I allowed myself to be held.

Legs up the wall pose

Legs up the Wall Pose

Yin Yoga teaches us balance. We harmonise the Yin with the Yang and the masculine energy with the feminine. The goal of the soul is to always get us back to a place of balance. We become clear on the choices we need to make to move us in that direction.

This pose means to me....

Everything.

Grace is always last cab off the rank and gets its valet parking ticket when we finally surrender to the back of the line. Of course it takes a lot of effort to get to that point and we exhaust all our other cabs first prior to receiving the 'Grace cab'. The driver of all the other cabs are usually operated by our ego which charge very costly fares by choosing the longest detours. Uber expensive! The 'Grace cab' finally comes when we need to drive away from the crash. A nervous breakdown, an accident, a loss, a divorce, an illness, an imminent death. A good old fashioned rock bottom.

Many teachings say that the greatest opportunities exist here – at rock bottom. When we feel completely powerless to change our situation and we give up the fight for control. I was broken and beaten and admitting defeat laying down my weapons at the feet of something bigger than me. I'm not sure I could have sunk any lower and been able to dig myself out. God must get sick of hearing 'help'. Just yell 'All hail the Grace Cab!'

When Hillary Clinton lost the election to Donald Trump she wrote:

'I prayed a lot. I can almost see the cynics rolling their eyes. But pray I did, as fervently as I can remember ever doing. Anne Lamott once wrote that the three essential prayers she knows are 'Help', 'Thanks', and 'Wow'. You can guess which one I reached for. I prayed for help to put the sadness and disappointment of my defeat behind me; to stay hopeful and open hearted rather than becoming cynical and bitter; and to find a new purpose and start a new chapter.'

The power of prayer is universal and has nothing to do with religion which is a manmade concept. The moment you allow the 'Grace blanket' to wrap its arms around you is the moment of sweet surrender.

Caroline Myss wrote this on the topic of grace:

'Grace strikes us when we are in great pain and restlessness. It strikes

us when we walk through the dark valley of a meaningless and empty life. It strikes us when our disgust for our own being, our indifference, our weakness, our hostility, and our lack of direction and composure have become intolerable to us. It strikes us when, year after year, the longed for perfection of life does not appear, when the old compulsions reign within us as they have for decades, when despair destroys all joy and courage. Sometimes at that moment a wave of light breaks into our darkness, and it is as though a voice were saying "You are accepted."

Yoga had a big role to play in my healing journey to find grace. A Yoga teacher said to me once that 'Wisdom is gained when a memory loses its emotional charge.' When you get beyond your own stuff. Your own fear. Your own pain. Then suffering becomes optional. And grace swoops on in.

Many people I have spoken to along the way have said 'Yoga literally saved my life.' The most successful recovery programs are based on helping the addicted person uncover a spiritual dimension whether that is God, higher power or the Universe. You begin to see the true self as the transcendent which supports the idea that your Intuition is your own medicine to healing. Yoga opens a doorway onto the path and into an ancient library of knowledge about 'life'.

Our modern world feeds off technology and information which is not the same as knowledge. Knowledge is based on truth whereas information is based on data. One stays the same and the other changes often. When you discover the truths from the ancient mystics before the age of computers and the world wide web there is a sacredness in that space. When there were no distractions, these yogis who walked the path before us learnt that wisdom comes from facing your pain.

In Yoga, the term used to describe our addictions is called *Samskaras*. These are the actions we take to alleviate our suffering that create imprints or neurological pathways in the brain that are very difficult to break.

Behaviour becomes a habit but the relief we feel is always temporary and never solves the original problem which is the underlying pain, trauma and abandonment from ourselves. The truth is, everyone has a place inside of them that is unimaginable and excruciating to touch so we lock it away. It is only through Yoga that we become opened to the possibility that we can open all the hidden compartments of shame and grief and trauma that is buried inside of us.

Yoga became my gateway drug to find my own medicine. The Yoga mat was where I found refuge. The word 'refuge' is defined as 'the state of being safe or sheltered from danger or difficulty'. I think the operative word here was 'safe' because my nervous system was stuck in a chronic fight or flight response to hidden trauma. I needed this place of ritual safekeeping. A place I could go to lay down my armour and put down the trauma so I didn't have to constantly haul it around with me. A place which was just for me and would accept my brokenness without me needing to speak. The mat became the one place I could return to and leave feeling a little more stable and balanced.

Each day took so much energy just to show up in pain and still do all the things. There were so many reasons for me to seek refuge. I craved the mat just like I craved the drug. Both provided exactly the same purpose, to provide a way in which to feel more spiritually alive. It's just funny which one finds us first. They often say recovered addicts make highly spiritual beings because they have the same desire, they just want to *feel* good. For the time being I was playing with both. The Yoga mat was just the one loving and holding me until I was strong enough to love myself and come off the medication.

CHAPTER 9

A MYSTERY

'I bend so I don't break'

Prayer was not something we practiced in our family. Prayer to me was only ever sung growing up to the tunes of Bon Jovi's 'Living on a Prayer' and Madonna's 'Just like a Prayer'. Religion was to me (and still is) an outdated patriarchal system. But as a ten year old girl, I started to wonder and become curious about the bigger world and craved a connection with the great mystery. I recall asking my mother if she could teach me how to pray. Like any loving mother she agreed and did her best. At bedtime before she would tuck me in, we would bring our hands together in prayer and recite 'The Lord's Prayer'

"Our father who art in heaven, hallowed be thy name"...

Now I had no clue what the words meant, but the ritual of it felt sacred to me. I was doing what I was born to do; communicate with the divine and acknowledge a greater power I knew intuitively lived inside of me. Even from a young age with no religious education I instinctively felt this was right and my little soul was happy. I'm not sure how long this nightly routine went on for, maybe a year, maybe less, but it didn't matter. What mattered was that I believed and experienced my intuition giving me the nudges to engage in a sacred ritual which came from a place of love. A place of great mystery.

I remember when I was ten years old and I was experiencing some sort of existential crisis. This seems young for a significant moment such as this but I had a wild imagination and was always creating stories and pretend scenarios that seemed real to me.

So it wasn't unusual for me to live between the physical world and the mystical world. I had experienced several pets die in my life already, so perhaps I was contemplating my own mortality during my childhood. As a result, I surrounded myself with an imaginary zoo of creatures. I had several invisible animal friends as a kind of backup system because I knew the likelihood that my furry family members would die was quite high.

The existential event which sparked this fascination was probably the death of our first family dog Bess. She was an airedale terrier and a very loyal and smart dog. When I was six, she would accompany my sister and I to the bus stop each morning on my way to school. She would happily trot beside us and ensure we got to our destination on time.

One particular morning as she ran along, I crossed the busy road to reach the other side where the bus stop was and alarmingly heard a horrific noise. It was the sound of howling mixed with whimpers of pain. Bess was hit by a car and broke her back while doing her daily duty of guiding us on a safe journey. That was her last day on earth. It was the first time I saw my father cry when we had her put down and the first time I was introduced to pet heaven. I was told her spirit would live on even though she was not physically here. I guess it was also the first time I thought about the fact we exist in two forms. One is made of flesh and bones and the other is made of spirit, soul and our own memories. Both forms are equally true but one is beyond our five senses. So my imagination of course wanted access to communicate with Bess and thus the first signs of my intuition were stirred. The name 'Bess' means *God is my oath*.

By this age I had also gone through several near death

experiences of my own due to my severe peanut allergy. My mother could never understand why I would walk around the house croaking like a cat with a fur ball in my throat after eating a peanut butter sandwich. It took my lips swelling up like 'Fat Albert' for her to pay attention. But avoidance of nuts was never enough, because you learnt as time went on, that peanuts could turn up in the most unexpected of places. Like the day I ordered a banana smoothie at the Eumundi markets and unbeknownst to my mother, the vendors threw in a handful of crushed peanuts. The surprise here being that because I was sucking it through a straw there was no lip service warning as it hit the back of my throat directly. Instead, an immediate blocked airway elevated me to the next level of urgency. I survived this incident and many more. Over the years I understood that breathing is not an option so naturally I became pretty curious as to what happens when you stop. The truth is nobody understands allergies and their prevalence now days just as much as nobody understands the rise in people with chronic pain. They remain medical mysteries.

When you have a chronic life threatening allergy the veil between the worlds can become very thin as each time you fall victim to an emergency reaction you think to yourself... *could this be it*? I grew up during a time before the safety backup of Epi-pens and 'no nut policies' at school. In fact, I was the only child in my entire primary school with this 'intolerance'. I knew I was different from the other kids and sometimes labelled a 'fussy eater'. At birthday parties I would rather have risked my own life and eaten sweets containing nuts than ask for a special meal. I didn't want to be inconvenient or labelled the weird one, but life had other plans for me. I was young and food was just the start of my attempts to control my environment and the potential threat it posed to me. It peaked during my final year of primary school when both parents were beside themselves with how to help me.

***

I have just turned eleven years old and I am sitting in a doctor's office. This man, Dr Potts, is wearing a brown tweed jacket and hides behind a bushy brown beard. He peers at me through a pair of brown rimmed glasses and looks at me with the same eyes that the vet expressed before putting down our dog Bess.

"If you don't eat you are going to die Christina," he says very seriously.

I stopped eating around six months ago after going to a music camp where I didn't really know anyone else and felt anxious and out of place. The food was also disgusting and inedible so it was easier not to eat. When I returned home my clothes were a little bigger on me and I quite enjoyed looking smaller. This marked the beginning of my rebellion against nourishing myself.

I look back at Dr Potts with wide eyes. My face is gaunt and grey and I weigh a tiny twenty-six kilograms. I don't answer so he continues.

"Christina, I am going have to admit you to hospital next week if you don't gain any weight. We will set a goal of one kilogram and I want you to try really hard to eat okay?"

The last thing I want is to go to hospital where I can no longer control what goes into my body. Medicine, IV tubes, fluid, calories crawling under the unsealed doors like gremlins attacking me through my bare skin. Anorexia captures me terrified and tied up. The doctor's fear-based strategy makes me worse and even more ashamed of eating. My mother pleads with me to take just one sip of a milkshake.

"C'mon Tina, just have half of it and that will be enough, please try!" she begs.

We sit at the kitchen bench for what feels like hours staring at this glass filled with fat. I cannot let it near my mouth. We sit in silence and the great stare off continues waiting to see who will draw a breath first. All I want is to be left alone except now I'm under surveillance and this is not going to happen. I can no longer pour the drink down the sink and pretend I had it. I can no longer throw my dinner under the house to my secret stash of discarded roast lamb, potatoes and spaghetti.

I learnt how to lie so well during this period of my life. It's my practice ground that programs me to grow up into the perfect addict. Everything now on my plate is being counted for and measured. A spotlight is shone on my shame and I shrink even further into an abyss. My mum is fragile and broken after already dealing with divorcing my father. The family is breaking up, she literally is empty of power and does what anyone would do when they are at a rock bottom. She picks up the phone and calls her own mother.

"Hi Mum, is it ok I bring Tina down to stay with you for a few days?"

My Nan at the time lives on the Gold Coast. There is something so comforting about her home I quickly settle into the guest bedroom and make a little home for my soft toys on the bed. She wakes up early every morning and I hear her pottering around in the kitchen. She likes to sip her tea in bed while reading the paper. A ritual she continues to do to this day at one hundred and one years old. When I wake up each morning I go into her bedroom and crawl in under the covers beside her. My Pop volunteers at the Coast Guard so has delivered her toast and vegemite to her bedside and left for work already.

"Hello love." She greets me the same every new day. I lay beside her and lift her jewellery box off the bedside table to rest on my lap. I like to open the lid and gaze at all her jewels and trinkets and beautiful grown up things. They stare back at me begging to be tried on. I pick up a shiny ruby ring.

"Nan, can I have this when you die?" I ask.

"Of course love'" she replies without even looking away from her paper. Nan doesn't force me to eat breakfast but I find myself picking up a piece of her toast and having a nibble. It tastes so good I take another bite. Nan smiles to herself.

"Do you want to help me with the garden today? It needs a good water" she asks.

"Okay," I reply.

By the evening she suggests a special TV dinner watching Young Talent Time together on her comfy reclining chairs. I request a plain bowl of macaroni pasta with no sauce and grated cheese on top.

"Okay love," she says.

A few days turns into a week and my Mum comes back to pick me up. For the first time in a long while she sees me smiling. My Nan being the exact healing balm I needed to turn around the aggression of the disease inside of me. Love healed me, fear did not. And it came to me on the back of a toilet door. Yep, on the back of the loo door at my Nan's hung a particular piece of writing which struck a note in me during this time. It was the '*Desiderata*.'

As I sat on the loo doing 'God's business' I would look at the words and read the whole thing from start to finish with every visit.

For some reason the opening words made me feel calm.

Go placidly amid the noise and haste, and remember what peace there may be in silence.

I gave myself the goal of learning it off by heart;

Speak your truth quietly and clearly, and listen to others

The most comforting line of all being;

You are a child of the Universe no less than the trees and the stars; you have a right to be here…it is still a beautiful world, strive to be happy.

The speed at which this eating disorder descended upon me was so intense nobody saw it coming. Luckily it turned around just as quickly as it arrived. I can only imagine now as an adult with my own daughters how my mother felt witnessing me being held captive by this dark force. It was even before I hit puberty so body image and looking thin had not yet arrived in my field of awareness. I don't know how it got to this point except that controlling what I put in my mouth became all I lived for. The outside world became an unstable and unsafe place. The alchemy to healing chronic illness here was found in the mystical realm of unconditional love.

You could say that coming face to face with death and your own mortality can turn your life upside down and be the best medicine to transcend pain and suffering. My father was humbled at only thirty-six years old when he had a serious heart attack and survived. Up until that day he had been a heavy smoker. A pack a day for twenty years kind of habit. The day he was discharged from hospital he threw his pack of cigarettes in the bin and quit cold turkey living another twenty five years. A serious health scare or a near death experience usually lands in people's lives on purpose. Mystically right on time to shake them out of addiction or destructive behaviour. To move them from fear and back to a place of self love and self acceptance.

Seated
forward bend

Seated Forward Fold

Quan Yin is the Goddess of Compassion. She embodies all the qualities of Yin Yoga and is considered to be the most beloved Buddhist deity. She is all about the deep medicine that comes simply from being able to hold our pain and suffering in total presence. She also can bear witness to somebody else's pain without trying to judge or fix it. Often, calm compassion is all that is needed to offer to heal and transform darkness to light.

This pose means to me...

Taking a deep bow into my own life and becoming curious about my inner world. It's not about touching my toes but about looking at the world from the inside out, rather than the outside in.

Pain is largely a mystical experience. It cannot be validated or measured outside of yourself. You can give it a rating out of ten but that is one hundred percent subjective and felt only by you. 'Feeling' being the operative word; beyond the control of the intellect. So comments such as 'it's all in your head' from outsiders and anyone who consider themselves an 'expert' in chronic pain, are not only unhelpful but totally untrue.

You can't think your way out of pain. It is not logical. If I asked you to bring me your pain in a box and show it to me, you couldn't. You cannot measure it like you can take a blood pressure reading or read a person's body temperature. It's all rather abstract in physical reality because you can't see it, so to shift it, you need to get beyond the physical world. You need to trust your own medicine through healing it energetically in the realm you cannot see.

One particular woman who explains this demonstrably is neuroscientist Dr Jill Bolte Taylor. A neuroscientist who had her own near death experience and suffered a severe left hemisphere stroke and lives to tell the tale as the subject of her own research. Having relied heavily on the left logical side of her brain for all her working life, she had to recognise her right side as an instrumental part of her own rehabilitation. Our right sided hemisphere is our creative, expansive and intuitive circuit which governs our emotional intelligence. If we limit our healing to western medicine and its left dominant evidence-based practices, then we deny half of our own biology. She writes from 'My Stroke of Insight':

'Sensory information streams through our sensory systems and is immediately processed through our limbic system. By the time a message reaches our cerebral cortex for higher left brained thinking, we have already placed a 'feeling' upon how we view that stimulation – is this pain

or is this pleasure? Although many of us may think of ourselves as thinking creatures that feel, biologically we are feeling creatures that think.'

This supports the idea that we are not humans having a spiritual experience but spiritual beings having a human experience. When emotional stress causes pain in the body, surely the cause is non-physical and would benefit from discovering what is blocking your spirit from flowing freely through the body. This includes going through the door of your consciousness, past traumas and emotions. Treating pain with physical pills has no real power because it is not a physical predicament. It simply Band-Aids the problem and puts a layer over it so your treasure becomes buried. The following story is a great example of the self excavation that needs to take place in order to realise your hidden jewel and find your power:

The story of the Golden Buddha

*In the mid 50s, a Thai monastery was to be relocated to make room for a new highway. The monks arranged for a crane to come and move a 10 feet tall clay Buddha to its new location. When the crane started to lift the statue, it was much heavier than expected and began to crack. Wanting to protect the priceless shrine, the monks lowered it back down and decided to wait until the next day to bring more powerful equipment. To add insult to injury, the rain came in, so the monks lovingly covered the statue with tarps to keep the moisture away. In the dark of the night, the head monk took his flashlight and went out to make sure the Buddha was adequately covered. When the light of the torch shone into the crack of the clay, he saw a glimmer....a reflection of something underneath that shroud of clay. He immediately started to carefully chisel away shards of clay to find the glimmer grew brighter. Hours later, when all the clay had been removed... he was in the presence of a Buddha made of solid Gold!**

*An excerpt from Jack Canfield's *'Chicken Soup for the Soul'*

The Buddha taught that we can access our own healer by visualising how a caring mother holds her beloved child. Love is our true nature, but it is often covered over by the protective layer of fear. The only way to uncover the gold is to chip away at all the layers of yourself. Through the mystery of YOU. And experiencing how to understand yourself at the deepest level as a spiritual and intuitive being. Over the course of my life, starting from when I was a child, I piled layer upon layer over this Golden Buddha. The heaviest layers contained my own collection of limited thinking and unconscious conditioning. The other layers were added on from external influences such as parents, teachers, employers, the media, the government and their collective cultural beliefs. Because of the shame and unworthiness I weighed myself down with, loving myself as an adult now became almost a rebellious act. It was the difference between a life lived actively and a life of passive floating. Taking responsibility for myself meant refusing to allow society to do my thinking, talking and deciding for me. Loving yourself is actually a threat to our culture. It means that you don't fall for shallow easy solutions, or stop treating your body as a commodity, or buy into superficial products you don't need, or agree to an unnecessary medical procedure, or vote for a particular party. No wonder we are all covered up with clay! It's much easier for the patriarchy to fool us when we don't consider ourselves to be precious and worthy. Adrienne Rich says...

'Once we begin to feel committed to our lives, responsible to ourselves, we can never again be satisfied with the old passive way'.

Eventually it took several detonations to explode me apart. The childhood eating disorder, the traumatic birth, the shingles illness, the drug addiction were all forms of dynamite used to discover my true pathway and expose the gold that was at my earth core the entire time. These types of crises or breakdowns are not something we should fear or ignore in our life because ultimately they are there to set us straight and tell us something much deeper. But unfortunately because our culture is shaped to avoid pain, to cover it up with clay, to suck it up and soldier on, hidden trauma can be life threatening if depression sets in and mental health is affected. When the gold stays buried and covered, the hole in your soul remains and you lose your power. Your unique energy or spirit, which is there to serve your soul, loses its purpose and shifts to another place. That 'other' place where your power goes stays a mystery until you find the mystical path.

***

It's around this time that I realise it is going to take a lot of courage to enter the path and find the 'other' place. Even though I am not taking pills anymore I still long to remove the lowest dose left of the Buprenorphine 'patch'. I have realised the powerlessness of my mind to heal this addiction. I'm letting go of the mental struggle to work this out because it's destroying me. If I could think my way out of addiction I would have done it by now. It is the mind that is sick and won't heal me here. I need to trust something else to manage my life. My intuition. I need to become unconditionally ready to meet the unknown and everything that has been haunting me. I need to face the truth.

The final layer of opium is the most stubborn layer of clay remaining on my Buddha. I don't need to try and turn the ghastly clay into gold, I just need to stage a rebellion and bust open the doorway to the mystic's treasure room of unconditional love. I need a holy troublemaker who is very comfortable with the mystical cave to guide me. Someone who can connect me with a power greater than my mind. Someone with very high spiritual self esteem who is not afraid to excavate the depths of the human soul where the real precious gems exist.

CHAPTER 10

THE HEALER

'Yoga is not for the flexible, it's for the willing'

My intuition guides me to see a Medical Intuitive looking for some deeper answers. After a Near Death Experience (NDE) this particular woman was pronounced clinically dead. She died for 45 minutes after a heart attack and returned to her body with insights and healing abilities which were supernormal. Unlike most regular healers she could access information on another level entirely from the quantum field of possibility. She could see auras and read people energetically as well as psychically and was very accurate in connecting to metagenic energy. I was willing to try anything to help me. The morning of our appointment I find myself quite nervous driving to her consulting rooms. Of course it is the 'unknown' factor of what might happen during a meeting with a 'medical intuitive' that has my heart rate beating a little faster.

"What will she do to me? Will she be able to read my mind?" I ruminate.

I arrive early and am waiting in the reception area when she comes out to find me. She is escorted by another woman who I later learn is there as a precaution to provide an instant psychic reading as a second opinion for all her new patients. I pass the test and am ushered into a darkened consulting room where there stands two lone chairs facing opposite each other. I am instructed to sit down and the healer sits directly opposite me, our knees facing one another. My heart rate continues to climb as I feel totally confronted and almost naked in front of her. Sensing my nervousness she makes a couple of light hearted remarks and admits to appearing quite 'kooky' and strange when people first meet her.

"Don't worry I'm used to it," she laughs. I didn't even say anything to prompt her! When she sits down we begin to chat casually at first and then she asks me why I am there.

"I have this chronic pain condition after getting shingles and I'm totally dependent on pain killers. I don't want to feel this pain anymore, can you help me?" I beg.

She asks me a bunch of questions which have nothing to do with where the pain is in my body or how long I've been taking the pills for.

"Describe your husband to me?" she asks, eyeing me carefully.

"Do you enjoy being a mother?"

She listens to my answers but her gaze has shifted as she diverts eye contact and starts staring behind me, above my left shoulder. She continues to do this as she speaks, looking everywhere except at my physical body. She then asks me if I have dental problems. I explain my gums are very sensitive and bleed a lot and that I think it's because of the medication.

After a few more moments she makes a few notes and puts them neatly away in my file sitting upon her lap. She then looks up and says, 'you appear vacuous.' Which translates to me being totally empty of life force. Three years of taking opiates for the pain has drained me of my spirit. The shame and guilt around taking these pills everyday has eaten me up. I am completely out of alignment with my soul values which are strongly trying to make me a whole person again.

"Your energetic field is so weak you must call your spirit back. It's gone walkabout," she warns.

"Your survival in this lifetime depends on finding it again. Do you mind if I give you a treatment now?"

I nod silently, unable to speak.

She then gets up from her chair and walks over to stand above me from behind. I stay as still as I can and after about a minute the most intense sensation grows inside me.

Everything goes dark for a few seconds and then suddenly it feels like I've begun floating above the chair. My whole body is filled with this warm burning electrical energy that is pulsing out of me so much so that I can no longer feel the boundary of my own skin. It's frighteningly powerful; I feel lighter than solid matter.

"Am I actually floating? What's happening to me?" I ask as I feel my physical structure shatter and dissolve into thin air.

"Just relax, everything is ok," she reassures me. The power strengthens and almost miraculously I am existing in a different form. It is euphoric and I don't want it to end. What I experience next is a spontaneous light energetic healing. She steps back away from my body and slowly walks back to her chair.

"That felt so amazing," I gush breathlessly.

"It's nice isn't it?" she replies kindly. I can't believe this is all she has to say; what just happened was really ineffable and impossible to put into words.

I am literally charged up and downloaded with universal energy that kickstarts my intuition and gives my system the jolt it needs so desperately. I look at the clock on the wall and realise an hour has evaporated. It is time to leave.

"The changes will happen slowly over the next few weeks and you may need to come back for another meeting but it is unlikely I'll need to see you again. The people I see again are usually those who deep down are not really interested in healing. They are more concerned with wanting to know why things happened to them the way they did. You will be ok. Goodbye."

And with that, our session is over.

***

I try to hold onto the feeling I am left with after seeing her by reading her social media posts. She writes about people who refuse to heal and often expresses frustration around the nature of the work she does. How frustrating it must be for someone who *knows* intuitively why. She said:

"The space between you and Spirit is but a single layer of electromagnetic energy. 'They don't answer because 'you' don't want to hear. You don't know the answer because you won't listen to your intuition. Spells don't work, chants don't work, demands don't work and sheer ignorance will never work. Your body and your soul are your metronomes, so listen to them (you). I'll never be fabulously well known or regarded because I refuse to capitulate to the nonsense and I don't give out magic hand signals to help the Ju Ju work. But I will give you the truth as I know it and as informed by four near death experiences. That's all I've got.'

At home, I pick up one of Caroline Myss's books. A well known Medical Intuitive full of practical knowledge and experience.

"Everything is energy before it descends into matter," she writes.

"All your unfinished business, traumas and emotional baggage eventually download into your tissues if you refuse to face them."

As I pondered how to begin the search for my spirit I wonder if this is why they call it a 'Spiritual Journey'? A way to describe moving from point A to point B. Point A representing 'broken you' and point B 'healed you'? Or is it named a journey because it's like a long road you must walk and collect all the fragmented and fractured parts and put yourself back together like a jigsaw. After a while you realise that the 'journey' doesn't actually have an end point. It is just that; a journey or a process and it becomes about the walk not the destination. I am on the path though, and now I'm on it, there's no turning back and only one direction to go - forward.

Tina Bruce

Dragonfly Pose

Dragonfly Pose

There is no right or wrong way of practicing Yin Yoga. The way you become an animal shape will not be the same as someone else's expression. In Yin Yoga we are not confined to alignment or trying to keep up with a class. There is less doing and a whole lot more being.

This pose means to me...

Stretching my spirit in preparation for dancing
and hovering over life's beauty.

Some scientists believe that a proposed theory for a Near Death Experience or an energetic experience of light healing, is that it increases the body's electromagnetic force field, stimulating the pineal gland, a tiny nodule deep in the brain that secretes hormones that influence the working of the immune system. I've always found it slightly annoying to read about other people's mystical experiences mainly because I wanted to experience them for myself. They all seem to repeat the same thing though which is that 'no words can describe it'. You will read many metaphoric descriptions that begin with 'It was like' because that is as close as you are going to get to understanding the real thing. However, there are various opinions amongst science and tradition that may help me communicate this.

The ancient yogis describe their Guru's touch as releasing the bound Kundalini energy coiled at the base of the spine which starts its journey upwards towards God. The stirring of this energy is called *Shaktipat* and is the internal medicine we are capable of creating once it is freed. *Shaktipat* literally means the 'descent of grace' and is usually transmitted in a physical blessing traditionally with a touch on the forehead or crown of the head. After the initial touch, an instantaneous download of divine energy and an awakening of the spirit within reclaims you to your highest nature. You will be motivated to practice again and again just to connect with it once more. Your intuition will grow stronger and stronger the more you learn how to trust it and access your own soul again so that you can experience this great power.

Whatever it is, I am happy to receive it from the medical intuitive healer and leave our meeting wanting more. Slowly over the course of the next year as I deepen my meditation sessions I realise I can access this energy again. They say even if you get the light for just a second it's enough for a whole lifetime and you will continue to follow it like a moth to a flame. The more I meditated the less I craved medication and the less pain I felt. I was slowly re-wiring my system with more light.

I was reclaiming my spirit from the past from parts of me that had already died in preparation for a new beginning in life. A resurrection of my spirit. I was slowly realising my wholeness and my holiness at the same time.

Dr Joe Dispenza describes it as....

'The We (consciousness) is the software that runs the computer (body), and because it is connected to the Internet (energetic field), it can always be upgraded. This is essentially what we're doing in meditation – upgrading our operating system. Sometime these updates happen incrementally and the changes are subtle and behind the scenes (eg. When you are sleeping). At other times, in moments of epiphany, revelation, openness or surrender, we can upgrade to a totally new version of the operating system (Being). So what is the mechanism used to connect the software to the Internet? Wi-fi (meditation).'

The mystery of your consciousness, your connection to something greater than your physical self is where the medical industry is at a crossroads with energetic healers. Scientific evidence is the gold standard in the western world but healing is a profession that is thousands of years old, long before double blind clinical studies.

Science, according to Google, is derived from the Latin *scientia* which means *'knowledge'*. It is defined as the study of the nature and behavior of natural things and the knowledge that we obtain about them. What is also really interesting is that *intuition* is defined as the ability to obtain *'knowledge'* based on feelings without the need for conscious reasoning. Both modalities have the exact same objective so it appears diving into the mystery is the next frontier in healthcare if we are going to evolve and become really *knowledgeable* on things.

Many doctors will still prefer to protect the status quo and fear embracing a new understanding. But shouldn't science be open for inquiry? I wonder what has happened to curiosity in medicine as the best doctors I have met are the ones who *know* what they *don't* know. Control has taken over from curiosity, certainly when it comes to women's health and reproductive rights. If healthcare can step away from the fear of 'I don't know' and go back to a beginners mindset we open up a new way of growth and integration. Not asking questions is anti-science.

So I'm dreaming now of a different way of medicine beyond 'five minute consulting' and unnecessary intervention. Something which calls in the sacred and honors our ancestral lineage and then combines it with science. The feminine is longing to be called into the masculine medical world and men need this just as much as women for their wellbeing too. Healers often feel hidden but we need their knowledge in healthcare too. Our system can't sustain itself the way it is going. Doctors need to acknowledge that there is something more. We have a sense of spirit and an energy anatomy that has to be recognised because it impacts so greatly on the dis-eases of the future.

If healthcare was based on the Taoist principles of wholeness wouldn't we look at healing in a completely new way?

What I have gained so far from merging both 'knowledge' worlds together......

Any chemical you put in your mouth in the form of an opioid pill just turns into liquid handcuffs inside the body. It alters your system in a particular way that adapts very quickly to your receptors and your system loses its ability to function without it. You give your power away to pills, reducing your existence to living in a smaller empty space, energetically vacuous and lifeless. That's not a drug for long term chronic pain, it's a prison sentence confined to a dark isolated cell. The medical and pharmaceutical industries know this now after it has become a global opioid epidemic of course. There is hope though. To adjust the lens from problem solving pain to preventive medicine requires a holistic approach.

I learned to look at the trauma rather than hide from it. And this took time. I had to learn to turn towards it and feel each pang of pain like it was a newborn baby in need of a cuddle. It's a difficult thing to sit with it, hold it, and be compassionate in its presence. Was I safe in my body? I had to be able to seek the comfort within. I had to treat my body like a sanctuary and create a home inside with a nice warm fire. I had to remind myself that the discomfort and the crying will settle when I pick up the baby and hold it to my chest. Your capacity to love and hold your pain and suffering like it is your own child is limited to your capacity to love and hold yourself. Being compassionate and gentle with yourself will get you much further than being your own critic. Remind yourself that you are doing your best and not to carry the burden on your own. Let the weight on your shoulders become a shared weight with those you trust. Trying to do it all on your own will just block your intuition because you are operating from fear. Being open to the love and support of those closest to you will open your heart ripe for healing.

I needed to lose the pain from my identity. It wasn't *my* pain but *the* pain. *The* pain was not personal. I only made it personal when I became afraid of it so there needed to be a sense of trust. Any time I slipped back into victim mentality and questioned why did things happen the way they did to me, the pain sensed the fear and got worse.

Meditate before you medicate. I realised that I had my own inner pharmacy. The more I meditated the easier it became to control the pain. In stillness and silence I produced my own natural opiates. Somehow the body knew how to heal itself. The other key finding in this research is that meditation and guided imagery increases the production of endogenous opioid – the opium like substances that the brain produces to erase pain. In other words, you have an inner pharmacy already totally equipped to manufacture your own drugs. You just need to know how to access them! Your brain is totally capable of producing the natural soothing balm and unlike medications they are non-addictive, and offer a much more effective high! To meditate becomes your daily devotional practice.

I realised I had the power to change my own brain. This is called neuroplasticity. As they say; *neurons that fire together wire together*. So scientists have now discovered that it is possible for the brain to unlearn this. Not by thinking about it, working it out or problem solving, but by using visualisation and meditation. It's not fixating on logic but rather stimulating the right side brain which houses your non-reasoning and creative side. There are now thousands of clinical studies that daily meditation produces changes in the brain that change pain signals. Research shows that the many of the parts of the brain that light up when processing pain signals are the same areas that process sensations, images, memories, emotions and beliefs. This explains why when we are in pain we can't think properly or make decisions clearly. And also why we feel more sensitive to noises and our environment and become emotional. Our neurons which regulate these responses become hijacked to fire the pain signals. They learn to do that over time as a feedback loop grows stronger between the brain and the body where the initial illness or injury took place.

I learnt to distinguish between my ego voice and my soul voice. Someone once said to me 'the spiritual life is like rowing a canoe away from a waterfall, if you stop rowing you are pulled backward.' I certainly didn't want to sink any further into the whitewash. Life already felt to me like a giant washing machine. Tumbling round and round gasping for a breath whenever possible. That's the merry-go-round of pain and opiates. Soul says, 'No don't numb me. Numbing me down is dumbing me down!' The ego screams 'Yes! Make it stop'. We need the pain to remind us to survive or else the sneaky ego would simply drown us down to the bottom of the waterfall. Leaving no air behind.

CHAPTER 11

INDIA

'If you can breathe you can do Yoga'

Where might my spirit be? Where was it hiding? It made sense to go to the birthplace of spiritual seeking and inside the sacred country of India. Namely Rishikesh, the Yoga capital of the world. Interestingly Rishikesh is known as the 'home of the Rishis'. The place where all the Hindu seers, great sadhus and sages marked on the map as a holy land. These mystics realised after intense meditation the supreme truth and eternal knowledge due to its geographical location on the banks of the sacred Mama Ganga river. I was ready to embark on a personal pilgrimage to go find the part of me which had mysteriously disappeared and 'yoke' it back into being.

"There is no coming to consciousness without pain.
People will do anything, no matter how absurd, to avoid facing their own soul.
One does not become enlightened by imagining figures of light,
But by making the darkness conscious."
Carl Jung

***

My plane lands in Delhi in the darkness at midnight. I find my luggage and make my way to a nearby airport hotel where I try and get a few hours' sleep before transferring to Rishikesh in the morning. The journey the following day involves an eight hour drive in a car directly north. Except driving in India is more like dodging. We weave in and out of rural towns between taxis, trucks and bikes all overloaded with cargo including bales of string, pipes, sticks, goats, and pilgrimage walkers.

We arrive to our destination late in the afternoon and the streets are filled with devotees both Indian and western tourists and seekers. I am terrified of monkeys after having a bad experience on pot when I was a teenager and deciding to watch a movie called 'Outbreak'. I bravely walk towards my hotel and look one foot away from me at a family of five monkeys all staring me up and down. I have no bananas hanging off me but they are known to swipe mobile phones so I consciously stop taking photos with my device. I find myself saying 'excuse me' to a cow which is blocking the path ahead.

Holy cow is a literal reality here. Populations of them wander about freely; walking into shops, causing traffic jams as they have the right of way every place they moo. Cow paddies are all over the place but also considered sacred. I later see a cow whose benevolent face is covered with runny poo and my heart goes out to it. I want to hand it a tissue. That's what this place does to you though. It opens your heart. I know I am ready to start my Yoga retreat in the art of Bhakti.

The teacher training course I was there for was in Bhakti Yoga, or Yoga of the Heart. Bhakti Yoga is known as the 'Yoga of Devotion'. It has been called "love for love's sake" and "union through love and devotion." Basically you throw yourself into all their spiritual practices and rituals through chanting and meditation to experience a oneness with everything. Not everyone's cup of tea but if you're a yogi this is definitely on the bucket list. In the west we are used to Yoga being a form or exercise or even a hot and sweaty workout. This could not be further from the truth in India. The physical practice is only one limb of an eight path philosophy. While traditionally many of the practices worship the Hindu deities, Yoga is not Hinduism and not all yogis are Hindus. In fact, religion has very little to do with it. The only thing that all religions have in common is that they all describe the same thing when they experience a union with God. It occurs in a meditative state and feels like an electric energy source that fills the whole body transforming you away from darkness and fear and towards light and love. Yoga also offers this potential to experience your own divinity and soul so you can be present with everything and move beyond your own mind prison.

I am there to break out of my pain prison and worship myself, and worship I do! Every morning at 7 o'clock I start my day down on the banks of Mama Ganga (Ganges river) adorned with my blanket and mala beads for a one hour meditation. Every time I sit down and close my eyes I see those five monkeys and am reminded of my *monkey mind*. Slowly and patiently I sit and continue counting my string of malas. After meditation and mantra we make our way to hot chai totally oblivious to the motorbikes and cars almost cleaning us up. Walking back to our hotel we pass Indian mothers so comfortably cross legged on the ground with their babies sleeping, bound to their bodies like little monkeys. We float past hundreds of Indian boys telling us to smile, rubbish everywhere, homeless saints, a goat, stray dogs, lots of poverty and beggars. It is an assault on the senses and not once do I ever feel unsafe. Just peaceful and strangely at home.

Even though I am amongst some of the poorest people and living situations, the locals are still rich in smiles and generous in spirit.

Even though I still feel the pain come and go, the pure vibration of the place lifts me out of it.

Even though I go to find my spirit, it finds me.

It finds me one evening on an auspicious New Moon holiday called the 'Maha Shivratri' which is a Hindu festival to celebrate the great night of Shiva. The Indian women around me are dressed up in their finest silk, arms laden with gold bangles and jewels embellished over their saris. There is the sound of jangling as they walk and gather together on steps and outside temples. They all have a sparkly Bindi in the middle of their forehead and are united in spirit and community.

The plan is to all meet down at the banks of the Ganga river for the Arttea traditional fire ceremony and chanting. Having rehearsed my mantras all week I am prepared to chant openly and amongst the festivities. Prior to coming to India my thoughts about chanting were kind of scary, and if I was honest, a bit cultish. It seemed like people had a general fear around using and expressing their voice anyway, let alone in the context of another language entirely and foreign country. But it is precisely because it is sung in Sanskrit that I am able to drop more into the vibration and repetition without engaging my thinking mind and it's constant search for meaning. Most people believe if they are not a professional singer why would they risk sounding like a loser in front of a group of people. But the Indians chant for pure joy and as a meditative practice and a way to feel connected to others. Mantra is their medicine. It's usually done in a call-and-response manner where one or a group of leaders sing one phrase and then you repeat it.

The ceremony begins and is accompanied by some incredible musicians playing the drums, gongs, tambourines and the uplifting electric sound of the harmonium all setting a slow tempo to start with. I slip into a comfortable rhythm and sway my body with the beat. It is impossible to sit still anyway as the collective vibrations move through my bones and shake me as I sing.

At the base of the Himalayas by the river, I repeat the chants over and over again and feel a warm familiar light pour into my being. I recognise it straight away. It is that frighteningly powerful energy I felt from the healer but it is coming from inside of me. I am generating this and it doesn't feel frightening at all. It is the source of my intuition and my own medicine filling me up from the base of my spine all the way to the crown of my head. It expands my heart and cracks me wide open to reveal the light within. My spirit has returned.

***

As I prepared to return home back to reality I picked up a book to read for the journey home. It was called *'A Goddess Amongst Us'*. It told the story of the life of *Anandamayi Ma.* She was a famous Hindu Indian Saint born in the late 19th century and was known as the *'Joy-Permeated Mother'*. She embodied the true essence of the divine feminine refusing to be called a 'Guru' so was affectionately known as 'Ma'. This was because she possessed a combination of the sweetness of maternal affection and the profound depths of the Mystical knower of the Goddess. It read....

'Her sweet smile held everyone spellbound and there was the profound sense of knowing her at a deep and eternal level, and a sense of being known by her from all eternity. Those who had met her felt as if they were meeting their very own after a long absence and were reluctant to leave her presence. Even people who were not interested in religion and spirituality were attracted to Ma as she awakened a deep spiritual longing in a completely natural and spontaneous manner in everyone.'

Why exactly did Ma captivate people's hearts then? Because her blissful states would inspire others to remember that aspect of their true Intuitive nature. Their own Mother's Medicine. She led by being the breathing example of *intuition* and living honestly and transparently through her soul.

I wondered if I could maintain this feeling of clarity and connection when I arrived home. Whether that little piece of India would stay in my heart. No matter how much chaos, craziness and change surrounded me as a mother, if I could trust my inner guru to follow my intuition, I would arrive at my own *'Joy-permeated Mother'*.

My experience in India was profound. It made the ghastly good again and turned it into gold. The gold was buried inside of me the whole time. The gold was my guru. And it was these words that sealed my spirit back into my body as I was ready to return home.

'I am my own guru.'

Easy Pose

Easy Pose

Ironically this pose earned its name due to its difficulty. We practice all the other shapes to help us sit physically still for meditation. Yin Yoga is the vehicle for healing as it opens up people's bodies first and then the mind and spirit follow. By resting and anchoring our mind on the sensations of the body we grow into our skin and become slowly more comfortable with being uncomfortable.

Easy Pose helps to develop a deeper awareness and offers a segue way into meditation.

What this pose means to me...

I meditate here to receive intuitive guidance and I pray to set intentions. Some people call it communing with God, talking and holy listening.

The Rishis refer to our intuition as the '*Buddhi*'. The *Buddhi* lives in the heart which is considered the organ closest to your soul. It has the largest energetic field and is like mission control for all your emotions. I knew this intellectually as a cardiac technician but never knew its real power. So I didn't have to believe it existed anymore because I actually felt and experienced my own spiritual power. And experience trumps belief. Belief is contained in the mind. It is logical and based on opinions whereas an experience is real and embodied. It is literally beyond belief.

One of the reasons I think that Indians are so happy is because they live in a culture where doubt does not exist even outside of their temples and ashrams. I really do believe that there are sacred locations on earth that open us up to expanded energies and an expanded sense of soul. I, like the ancient Saints and Sages and Sadhus, felt there was some greater power at work here. Clearly this idea did not originate from me though.

These mystics have absolute faith in a higher power because their daily rituals supported their experiences. And it was the moment I realised that I didn't need to seek or give power to things outside of myself when I understood that I had it *in* me the whole time. My highest power was already inside me. I believe it is available to anyone and at the crux of it all, the solution to all suffering is this spiritual connection. I'm pretty sure anyone who has tried to solve an inner problem by outer means has come to the same revelation. It's a universal truth. That us humans are, by design, our very own healers. Your Mother's Medicine comes from a vibration of love and when we are in that state, our pathway to healing is loud and clear. I also felt that to truly transcend my pain I had to become my own guru. It's just like the Good Witch Glinda from The Wizard of Oz says:

"You've always had the power my dear,
you just had to learn it for yourself."

Plenty of seekers travel the world looking for their 'Glinda' or an enlightened being to help them transcend their suffering. The word *guru* is made up of two Sanskrit syllables. The first means 'darkness', the second means 'light'. A guru is believed to demonstrate moving out of the darkness and into the light. The obsession of finding a guru however can distract you from the real truth that your healing comes from inside of you, not from external means.

There is of course, the incredible experience of actually being in the presence of a real live guru. I felt this high when I was standing only two meters away from Swami Chidanand Saraswati outside the Parmarth Niketan Ashram. His state of grace and pure divine power drew me in like a magnet. All of his energy from his enlightened body poured out of his eyes when he deliberately fixed his gaze upon me so as to see straight into my soul. It's like with a single stare he could cut through all that is not true and see me for what I really was; eternally at peace. So I received his x-ray vision and understood it was all contained inside of me. But to live from that place of connection twenty four hours a day? To embody it when my kids were arguing and the house was a mess and there were emails to answer and jobs to be done? I was most definitely going to need to work at it and bring home with me an unwavering spiritual practice.

An old Hindu legend tells of an ancient time when all human beings were Gods. But the people so lacked appreciation of their divine nature that the other Gods decided to take it away from them. Brahma, the supreme God, wanted to hide human divinity where people would never find it again and asked his fellow God friends to help him find the best place. One God suggested that they bury human divinity deep in the earth, but Brahma thought they would surely dig deep enough to find it again. Another God wanted to sink it into the depths of the greatest ocean, but Brahma thought that humans would eventually learn to dive deep enough to find it and take it up again. Another God suggested they store it at the top of the highest mountain, but Brahma knew that people would eventually climb high enough to conquer every peak on Earth. Frustrated, the council of Gods decided that there wasn't a single place on Earth that humans wouldn't know and conquer, eventually.

So Brahma himself began to think of ways to hide human divinity. He thought for a very long time. Finally, he said, 'we cannot hide their divinity on Earth for they are determined to own all of the planet. But if we hide their divinity within their own being, they will never think to look for it there.'

We humans have been looking for our divinity ever since.

Why do Mothers need to retreat?

It is not a simple task for mothers to leave their families for a weekend let alone a week. These rapid changes in our time have seen along with it a rise for the need for both mothers and fathers to gain permission to exit their ordinary lives and the accompanying chaos. The responsibilities we all face in this modern world are so intense that it is changing us from the inside out. We are the first generation of parents to be raising children in the digital age, which has not only increased the speed at which our kids are learning and developing both physically and mentally, but also demanded that we 'parent' faster.

Our wellbeing is being affected by the pressure of scheduled activities and screen time. We are facing resistance from our children every day as we have become monitors of their online life more than their offline life. And it is to our detriment. We are paying a big cost in terms of our overall health being in balance. So managing this dynamic has simultaneously created the longing for mothers to restore their energy. To grow and evolve their spirit so that have the stamina to be not just be 'mother monitors' but engaged and present 'loving mothers'.

My purpose in this life is to teach people how to slow down and listen to the voice of their soul. A retreat will get you beyond your five senses and all the external distractions of domestic concerns so that you can dig deep and hear your soul voice again. Mystical soul-size questions such as 'What does my soul need?' and 'Am I blocking my intuition?' 'What are my values and how have they changed in the last year?' Because you are not the same person that you were last year. So much has happened and shifted that you really need to insert a pause button just to examine your own life.

Soul-sized questions aren't really logical questions so you will have a hard time 'thinking' about the answers. They require some sacred listening and time to explore the inner cave of your heart. Because buried deep beneath all the responsibilities and roles you play is a hidden jewel. It might be surrounded by dust and layers of dirt but it is there. Yearning to be polished so you can shine.

A retreat is not a place to go to solve a problem. It is an opportunity to examine why things are a problem to you in the first place. This type of exploration may require you to ask yourself questions such as 'Help me understand what it is I am doing which is creating this problem or this road block or this pain?' 'What destructive subconscious programs are running my behaviours and choices?'

Retreats will reveal truths about you and course correct your path so that the direction you are walking towards is back to a state of balance. Back towards your higher self. Not your buried and over burdened mothering self. 'Mothering' is *what we do* but it is not necessarily *who we are*. To prioritise your soul is an act of self love which actually vaccinates your own children against low self esteem. My kids have observed me going off on retreat every year since they were toddlers. It excites them when I go away as they get to hang out with Dad and enjoy more lunch orders. I can only hope they follow my example as they grow.

Revelations, 'Aha!' moments and transformations are the result of guidance and insight you receive when on retreat. When you nurture your mystical mother, you understand your nature. When you understand your nature, you make better choices, you become inspired or 'in spirit'. When you create the right space the light can find you in the form of ideas, clarity and even the power of Grace as you experience the feelings of awe and wonder again. How you prioritise your soul will depend upon the unfolding of your own life events which will create certain needs and desires to act on it. As a sensitive child, and now an even more sensitive adult, I find it difficult to ignore the uncomfortable feelings and pain in my body. It's usually a pretty clear sign that something is off and I need some time out.

Traditional retreats were often in silence or in Buddhist monasteries. This has clearly changed as we have adopted these experiences to suit the modern woman. Comfort, luxury, spa treatments and connection with friends are now the abundant qualities that the modern woman is attracting. As well as doing the inner work retreats can now be pleasurable! This excites me the most because mothers in particular need to feel good if they are going to go home and give. And one of the best parts about retreating is that you can ease up on your mental load as every decision for you in terms of your schedule has already been curated and crafted on your behalf to offer you the most incredible experience of YOU.

When you leave a retreat you know how to honour your mystic mother. So that when you return to regular life, you can put yourself in a retreat space as needed in your own home. Because there will be a day when you wake up and you will need a quiet day of reflection so fill it with the things that fuel your soul. You leave knowing what the elements of that day require whether that is includes Yoga, meditation, journaling, bathing ritual, massage or a long walk and how to set it up like that. Some people may call this developing a home practice, I like to call it Mother's Medicine.

CHAPTER 12

BENEATH THE BAND-AID

'Be mindful even if your mind is full'

When is it time to rip off the Band-Aid? When the wound has healed is the common sense answer. During the twelve months of wearing 'the patch', my investment of all my energy into the journey fed and nourished my intuitive muscles. Along the way there were big questions I needed to ask like 'What do I believe is true about myself?' and 'Why do I do the things I do?' 'Why am I so afraid of suffering?' After all, we arrive into the world in great pain and we will most likely die and exit the world in pain. It is a natural part of life. I'm not afraid of death, the final moment, the last inhale, but I am afraid of *how* I'm going to die. Rip it off fast and while I'm not looking is how I would prefer this transition.

There was a particular time during a family holiday recently when we witnessed death and departure in between happy hour drinks and dinner. Staying at a hotel on the beach in Greece, on a little island called Naxos, we are relaxed and sitting back on our banana lounges. From our veranda I'm looking directly out at the Mediterranean Sea and the sun is reflecting off the surface like laser beams. Greece knows how to embody beauty on earth very well and shows off to us every day, putting on a spectacular display of pristine gloriousness. It is breathtaking to see how ancient and unspoiled the beach looks on this humble and unpopulated island.

We are one of only four families staying here as it is September which is end of season for the tourists. We are certainly the only Aussies here; the remainder being Europeans from the mainland who visit here every year on holidays. Just before sunset we routinely go for a wander down to the shore and walk around looking for natural things to collect. There are no seashells where we are but instead the sand is filled with beautiful smooth pebbles and rocks of every colour and shade of earth.

I signal to the girls that it is time to go down to the beach exploring before dinner so we take off barefoot and step delicately over the uneven surface to cross the dirt road. I watch them skip along calling out to the resident dog to follow us. I merge closer to the shoreline and then notice a group of people gathered about one hundred meters along towards the point. There seems to be someone lying on the ground and a crowd of five bystanders circling around. One young lady in a red bikini starts running towards us and waving her hands in the air. She is yelling something but I can't quite work out what she is trying to say. I then observe that the person lying on the beach is an older woman who is not moving. There is someone crouched over the top of her on their knees performing CPR. The girls innocently see the commotion.

"Let's go over there mum," one of them says. The young lady running towards me now starts signaling to me with her hands warning me to prevent the children from getting any closer and witnessing the event.

"Stay here girls," I say sternly.

"Nooo... we want to see what's going on," they plead. The girls don't understand so I explain to them that it looks like a woman is sick and unconscious and that we need to give them some space so they can help her. The hotel staff have now seen what is going on and are moving quickly to communicate with the lady in the red bikini. The hotel manager puts her hand to her forehead.

"She is a guest at our hotel!"

The ambulance is on its way but being such a remote part of the island it is likely to take some time to arrive.

"She is staying here with her son," the manager informs. Apparently the son is still windsurfing out in the ocean in front. We look out to the horizon and see him in his blue board shorts cruising about two hundred meters out. Now we have something to do. I tell the girls to start waving their arms around to get his attention. There we all are jumping up and down like jack in the boxes pointing towards his mother with some urgency. He finally looks over repeatedly and nods making his way in that direction. The wind is not co-operating and it is taking a long while to travel inland.

Half an hour passes and it's not looking likely the woman will be resuscitated considering the drowning was isolated and nobody knows how long she was submerged for.

"I want to go over and help Mum," Leila says. The son finally gets to shore and he drags his board up on to the beach and steps over the rocks. He walks over to his mother and drops to his knees beside her knowing her final breath has been taken. I tell the girls we need to get back to the hotel, keen to give the family some privacy.

Feeling a little shaken and overwhelmed I see the other guests standing around concerned.

"Is she dead Mum?" Zoe asks me.

"Yes, it looks like she might be," I reply matter-of-factly. After forty-five minutes the ambulance reaches its destination and the two paramedics make their way to the woman. We learn from the hotel staff that she is around eighty years old and passed away suddenly while taking a dip at sunset on her favourite beach. As we sit down for dinner that night we see the ambulance officers approaching the hotel after they have loaded her body into the back of the truck. The son meets them standing outside reception and they exchange documents. He is handing them his mothers' passport and in return they hand him a document. The bill for the service. A death transaction.

The following day, I am feeling a pressure build inside of me to do something to mark the death of this woman in a respectful way. An energetic force is rising and it overcomes me and motivates me earlier than usual that morning. I suggest to the girls that we go back to the beach and make an offering. Perhaps we can create some earth art out of stones in her memory. So we head back and arrive at the scene where the rescue happened. Marked on the ground is a giant drag mark from the shore to the back of the ambulance where her body was pulled along, creating a trail in the sand. A trail that will be washed away by the rising tide later that evening. We begin to collect and design our earth art in the shape of a giant love heart. Rocks of all shapes and sizes are placed in position holding the ancient secrets of thousands of years washed up and eroded away from another time and place. Who knows where they have come from and how they have formed our planet. The moment is filled with a tranquility and quietude and I ask Zoe

"What do you think happens when you die?"

She replies, "Oh, you just go up to the sky and choose what you want to be next. You know, like a tree, or a leaf, or an angel or an animal. Just like Grandpa Eugie is an eagle."

"Yes, I think you're right Zoe," I smile. My soul feels full. I want them to know that there is beauty in death but they already seem to understand. They see the love and know that there is something much greater beyond trauma, pain and suffering that holds us all in great reverence. The woman's heart stopped suddenly swimming in her favorite ocean at sunset. Pretty golden.

***

Arriving home from Greece, I am tired from the journey but have a renewed sense of hope that often lingers after a spectacular holiday. That feeling you just don't want to end but instead, want to share with others so you can re-live it again and again.

'The Patch' is now hanging off my skin and once again I am faced with the reality of slipping right back into routine and returning to my doctor to refill my script and replace it. The mere thought of depending on this medication is disheartening and I shut it out of my mind so it doesn't spoil my holiday bubble. A reminder alert pops up on my phone and I look down to see that I had booked to attend an event that evening. It is a gathering of like minded women joining in a circle to meditate, chat and share stories.

"Divine timing - an evening of connection is just what I feel like," I think.

I enter the room with no expectations and recognise nobody. My jet lag and anxiety is making itself known so I make a cup of warm tea and cradle it in the palms of my hands. I see the cushions on the floor shaped in a circle and walk over to choose a spot where I can sit and relax. As the teacher begins the opening and sets the tone for the gathering we all close our eyes and follow her voice as she guides us through a visualisation journey into nature. Straight away my attention is on the beach in Greece and it is like I can feel the sand underneath my body. And then just as quickly, intense thoughts of the darkened doctor's waiting room steal my thunder and take me out of bliss and right into heart thumping palpitations. I try to take a few deep breaths but the more I try, the harder it is to inhale any air at all. There is sweat dripping from my arm pits and I wonder if I am wearing any deodorant. My eyebrows are knitted at the centre and I am clenching my jaw like I am trying to squeeze the negativity out of my nose. My stomach is cramping and I feel a build up of gas in my belly from the long haul flight.

"I hope I don't fart - that would be so embarrassing," I think as I tense everything including my butt. I can sense the gloomy waiting room and visualise behind my third eye the faded posters on the wall of heroin help lines and bare arms with track marks and tourniquets.

I want to yell 'FUCK' really loudly in my mind as if I have some silent form of tourette's syndrome. My swollen ankles are now numb and the pins and needles in my feet are burning holes through the floor. I cannot keep my eyes shut to this nightmare any longer and suddenly the teacher says:

"Let's all bring our awareness back into this room and gently open our eyes."

I look around and there are women looking calm and still gently smiling to one another. I want to excuse myself and go straight to the bathroom where I can flush this panic attack down the loo. I am stuck to the floor though in a frozen frightened response. I can feel my face burning bright red and keep my gaze low so to avoid eye contact with anyone.

The teacher offers an opportunity to go around the circle and say what we are grateful for. I understand the intention around this exercise is to create connection but I am shaky and don't know if I can speak when I can't even swallow properly. I sip my tea gingerly and listen to the other people in the room. Slowly, I begin to tune into the gratitude stories and a few shared laughs loosen up the energy and my own anxiety. One woman bravely confesses, "I can't find anything to be grateful for."

Suddenly my eyes look up and I am fixated on her vulnerability and courage.

"My husband died last year, I have been diagnosed with Crohn's disease and I don't feel like my life has any meaning. I'm not coping and my boss bought me a ticket to come here tonight because he thinks it might help me," she says.

Tears are falling down her cheeks and she wipes the mascara from under her eyes with her fists. She doesn't bother to use the tissue sitting beside her. We all listen respectfully and I feel immense compassion pouring out of my heart towards her. The sacred space is holding her together, just. I hear her story and recognise her pain. It is starting to shift something inside of me making me feel less alone and isolated in my nervousness. As I am witnessing this woman in her rawness I feel a human connection beyond words. It is visceral and like a pressure rising inside of me, it urges me to open my mouth and I speak the words.

"You are not alone."

"I'm addicted to opiates. It's been hiding out in my bloodstream for three years and I want to let it go."

My voice is shaking but I continue to talk. Growing and strengthening my soul's expression with each sound I continue speaking. I feel the darker nastier parts of my psyche slowly evaporating with every word I utter. The voices that crave numbing and dumbing my pain in the dark shadows are being weakened by all the higher vibrations and positive energy that is circulating around the group.

"I'm afraid of the pain I will feel if I stop taking it but I don't want to numb myself anymore. It's just bullshit. I'm so over it. I don't want to feel like this victim. I just want to be present with life. With my girls. With me."

Nobody in the circle tries to fix my problem, or offer advice, or cheer me up, or give me therapy, or even a tissue - they simply listen. I take a big breath and sense the relief spread across my chest and lift off my shoulders. The shame has been shared. I had thought I could negotiate my addict alone and in private but at that moment I realise that my addict voice is losing power.

The next morning comes and I am finally ready to rip off 'The Patch' forever. My nervous system has me at knifepoint. I am so familiar with this drill and my ego is having a field day filling my head with all the doubts it can muster. Without this drug slowly leaking into my system who am I? I create a story to keep the pattern alive. I've had a bad day, or I'm overwhelmed or I deserve it or I'm coming down with something. I feel unsafe inside my own body without this superficial layer of myself. It only gives me a false sense of feeling safe though. As Buddha would say my attachment to it is merely 'an illusion'. Numbing, I discover, is only skin-deep. It covers you up in a warm blanket but underneath it all, the pain is still there, just in a smaller space.

Feeling fear still lurking inside of my body, I have that oh so familiar feeling of not enough. Not enough time, not enough space, not enough success, not enough energy. But what is lacking in me? What will it take to fill the void and to become 'enough'? When I rip off the band-aid will I be enough in all of my pain? Can I love my hurts enough to be with them without trying to soothe them from the outside? I know for sure now that I am worthy of love and belonging. The power of this truth takes time to fully understand. Worth is not given to us. It is not something we need to earn, it is claimed. I am strong enough and ready to claim it all in my power.

I silence myself in a meditation. I go to my prayer chair and close my eyes to shut down the outer world for a moment. Just long enough to tap into my own strength and conviction that I can do this. I settle into the world behind my eyes and make a conscious intention to shift from my addict voice to my more reliable soul voice.

"I have made a decision I want to live in this world emotionally unconditionally. I want to meet the world on its terms from now on. I know it's going to be painful but I want to be present to everything. Please help me weaken my cravings and give me the grace of fortitude and unconditional love. Guide me to make the right choices and keep me in my heart." I pray.

Quietly I tune into the world behind my eyes and listen. It doesn't take long for the following message to download:

"I will give you a soul chance on life, but only on one condition. You take my hand and choose to walk away knowing that you don't know what will happen. Except that I've got you. Come with me. I will show you how to do this. Trust me."

Who is that talking? I'm not sure whether I should trust a voice that is so unassuming yet expressing itself with such authority.

This voice is announcing itself in the dark, in silence and from a tiny spark in my heart. This voice is not speaking words so I am trying to understand its language. It's a knowing. An absolute certainty. I can feel it in my bones. It's a voice we are never taught to find because in finding it, we cannot go back to the shallow depths of who we thought we were. My intuition is leading me back to the pot of gold at the centre of my heart. And it is brimming with my own medicine.

Butterfly
Pose

Butterfly Pose

Every Yoga pose offers healing for the mind and body and an opportunity for spiritual transformation. Just like every day is a chance to start a fresh. The spirit feels like hope and the soul feels like truth. Perhaps the *Butterfly* is proof that you can go through a great deal of spiritual darkness and still become a beautiful soul?

This pose means to me....

Worshipping all the divine feminine parts of myself
with patience and compassion until
I'm ready to unfold and fly.

I have revealed my heart in this book because I know I am not alone. The way mothers connect meaningfully in all aspects of their lives is not through gossip or perfection or public displays of 'I'm fine'. The village of women is formed through vulnerability, failing, and sharing our fears. It's formed through the brutal honesty and laying down of our armour. I hope by me being 'ugly' honest it reassures you that you are not alone in your thoughts. I hope you can see your own story in my story as we all struggle to some degree with our own trauma, our own addictions and our own self-acceptance. If we share our story with someone who responds with empathy and understanding, shame cannot survive.

According to Brene Brown's research, here are the first three things that you need to know about shame:

1. We all have it. Shame is universal and one of the most primitive human emotions that we experience. The only people who don't experience shame lack the capacity for empathy and human connection.
2. We're all afraid to talk about shame.
3. The less we talk about shame, the more control it has over our lives.

Shame is basically fear of being unloveable – it's the total opposite of owning our story and feeling worthy. In fact, the definition of shame that developed from my research is:

> *Shame is the intensely painful feeling or experience of believing that we are flawed and therefore unworthy of love and belonging.*

What I have learnt from all of this is that underneath my Band-Aid was pain and underneath my pain was some form of fear. Pain ended up being an opportunity and a blessing to feel what fear was bringing up inside of me. Ultimately the more I embraced my fear, the less it dominated my experience. Anything that I embrace no longer has any power over me. And so the more I can face my natural fear the less it rules my choices.

By shining a light on the fear in your subconscious mind and holding it in consistently, it begins to burn and destroy it. Just like vampires are allergic to sunlight, what sucks your blood and what drains your life force is also destroyed by your own inner light. It only takes one strike of a match to light up a darkened room.

Learning to love ourselves is more about remembering than acquiring new knowledge. Becoming your own healer requires some spiritual sweat and a daily practice of tuning into your intuition. But it is available to all and the capacity to embody love in our bodies is not reserved for the elite or enlightened. It is so ordinary and mundane that we simply forget. We just need to remember that pain is a form of divine love essential to our birth into this human life. Pain is love. It is visceral and perhaps the deepest expression of love. So many of us fear being fully present in the body because it means owning just how painful we are. The responsibility is overwhelming.

There is nothing more powerful than a woman who has met with the truth inside of her. Knowing self love is knowing the soul. Love is innate and inherent in all of us. It is our birthright. My own divine worth from within was where all the answers were waiting for me. Inside the inner chambers of my heart the butterfly was waiting to break free. I may not have had the birth experiences I wanted but the truth is I look at my girls now, aged eight and nine and I am in awe of how I created them. I can fully own the fact that I made them.

Regardless of how they entered into the world, I still did it.

And I own it.

I made the ghastly good again and turned it into gold.

I am my own guru.

A LETTER TO MY DAUGHTERS

Dear Leila and Zoë

I promise I won't protect you from pain

I promise to teach you that you are strong enough to handle all of life's challenges

I promise to not shield you from the truth

I promise I won't edit information from your life

I promise I will be here for you when you need to be held

I promise that you will feel great discomfort but you can choose not to suffer

I promise to teach you how to pray

I promise to show you that the divine exists within your heart

I promise to lead by example and demonstrate that intuition can be trusted

I promise that your body is perfect the way it is and can perform miracles

I promise you don't need to change to please other people

I promise you have everything you need inside of you to belong

I promise that you are your own guru

I promise the more you love yourself the more love you
can give and receive

I promise you are enough.

ACKNOWLEDGEMENTS

Somehow this story is both ancient and current at the same time. It was me who wrote it but it came from a place of far more mystical origins. I knew this book was pregnant and growing inside of me but I kept it hidden for many years. It wasn't until I began to experience 'baby brain' again that I knew the birth was imminent. Unable to focus, to see clearly or get over my exhaustion my intuition was screaming 'it is time these words come out'.

I was confused because I'm an impatient and irritated reluctant writer. I enjoy being a storyteller but the task of sitting down to 'work' puts me off. I pretended not to hear the calling, but when ignored, this avoidance simply resulted in a slow disintegration of my senses. I was entering into madness.

So I did what I do best when in the void and went on a retreat. Time away from regular life and domestic responsibilities allowed the silence I needed to hear the voice.

"Forget the story Tina. What does it mean and what are you going to DO with it?"

I knew in that instant that this book that was asking to be written was not about me. The message was bigger than myself. If I tried to take on the responsibility all on my own I would surely collapse in fear and intimidation. I remembered when I was at my lowest point, a desperate mother in a pain prison and stuck on drugs, I just wished and longed to find someone who was going through something similar so I wouldn't feel so alone. Then I understood my purpose was to serve those women. This is my story but it is also *our* story.

Within two days I was sitting at my desk in the hotel room and the first chapter poured out of me in three hours. The process of putting it on paper created a healing of its own.

Fast forward four months and the first draft was done. Sounds very simple but it was a very intense period and came through me with much urgency. I had written the book like I was sitting on hot coals. It burnt its way through me destroying old traumas, past lives and karmic memories in its destruction. Creating the clean slate for renewal and rebirth.

Most evenings Oliver would return home from work and there I was hammering away at my computer. He would say "You are a bit obsessed, can you put it away and be present?" He was definitely correct. I was not just obsessed, I was possessed. The force was not going to release its grip until the job was done.

So I'd like to start by thanking Ollie. What can I say? Twenty years together. You have been the husband, the father AND the mother of our family. Showing up for me in steady ways I never knew I needed. Giving me the advice I never want to hear which is the sign of a true soul partner. We help each other grow. I love you darling.

Leila and Zoe who set me on this path and made me into a mother. You both cracked me open and gave me the strength to heal. I am so honoured to be your Mama and hope I can make you proud.

A big thank you to Vanessa Barrington of 'The Right Remark' for holding my hand and being both my editor, friend and magic word wizard. I know you didn't realise what you were in for when a dear friend introduced us both. Except that you agreed to hop on board and enjoy the wild ride with me! There is no way I could have produced this book alone so thank you for your guidance, being patient and knowing exactly how to gently nudge me in the right direction.

To my talented and creative artist Hannah Sutton, who has been with me from the very beginning of my journey. Designing my logo, my first blog, my Yoga cards and illustrations and quotes and now my first book cover. You draw so exquisitely and I am excited to be able to show more of your work through this book. You are incredible.

To my teachers. There are too many to name but every Yoga class counts. I know this and learn something new every time I get on the mat. Deep bow and Namaste.

To my doctors and healers. Especially to Paloma. You got to the root of my addiction to the pills right away. You prevented me from having to leave my family and go to rehab. Your service to your patients is remarkable and honourable. Forever grateful.

My circle of strong women, who always offer unwavering support and sisterhood. Especially to those who have showed up to my classes week after week. Who have witnessed me first telling my stories and held me in love even when my voice was shaky. It has been a privilege to start many of you on your own Yoga journey and watch lifelong friendships grow in our community.

To my mother, Thea. I am strong because you made me. It is no coincidence that your name is Greek for '*Goddess*'.

To my Nan, Nina. I am strong because you made my mother that way. It is no coincidence that your name is native American for '*Mighty Warrior*'. You are a survivor.

And finally to every woman who has ever dared to face her vulnerability. If you have read this far, thank you. And if you are still struggling in pain I want you to know you are not alone. And that everything is going to be ok. You are being watched more than you know.

I salute you.

www.ingramcontent.com/pod-product-compliance
Ingram Content Group UK Ltd.
Pitfield, Milton Keynes, MK11 3LW, UK
UKHW021840270726
14058UKWH00002B/262